OCCASIONAL PAPER 236

Lessons from the Crisis in Argentina

Christina Daseking, Atish Ghosh, Timothy Lane, and Alun Thomas

INTERNATIONAL MONETARY FUND

Washington DC

2004

© 2004 International Monetary Fund

Typesetting & Production: IMF Multimedia Services Division

Figures: Theodore F. Peters, Jr.

Cataloging-in-Publication Data

Lessons from the crisis in Argentina / Christina Daseking ... [et al.] —
[Washington, D.C. : International Monetary Fund, 2004].

p. cm. — (Occasional paper, 0251-6365) ; 236

Includes bibliographical references.

ISBN 1-58906-359-7

1. Argentina — Economic conditions. 2. Argentina — Economic policy. 3.
International Monetary Fund — Argentina. 4. Financial crises — Argentina.
I. Daseking, Christina,1964– II. Series: Occasional paper (International
Monetary Fund) ; no. 236.

HC 175.D37 2004

Price: US$25.00
(US$22.00 to full-time faculty members and
students at universities and colleges)

Please send orders to:
International Monetary Fund, Publication Services
700 19th Street, N.W., Washington, D.C. 20431, U.S.A.
Tel.: (202) 623-7430   Telefax: (202) 623-7201
E-mail: publications@imf.org
Internet: http://www.imf.org

recycled paper

Contents

Figures

Preface

In 2001–02, Argentina experienced one of the worst economic crises in its history. A default on government debt, which occurred against the backdrop of a prolonged recession, sent the Argentine currency and economy into a tailspin. Although the economy has since recovered from the worst, the crisis has imposed major hardships on the people of Argentina, and the road back to sustained growth and stability remains long. The events of the crisis are all the more troubling in light of the fact that Argentina was widely considered a model reformer and was engaged in a succession of IMF-supported programs through much of the 1990s.

This paper examines the origins of the Argentine crisis and its evolution up until early 2002. It analyzes the economic forces leading up to the crisis and draws general policy lessons, both for countries' efforts to prevent crises and for the IMF's surveillance and use of its financial resources. The review was prepared by a staff team under the general guidance of Timothy Geithner, former Director of the Policy Development and Review Department. The staff team comprised Timothy Lane (Assistant Director, Policy Review Division), Atish Ghosh, Christina Daseking, and Alun Thomas.

The authors are grateful to George Anayiotos for his contributions at the earlier stages of the project, to Sibabrata Das and Ivetta Hakobyan for research assistance, to Olivia Carolin and Sylvia Palazzo for secretarial assistance, and to numerous colleagues at the IMF for detailed comments on the paper. Jeff Hayden of the External Relations Department edited the paper and coordinated production of the publication.

An earlier draft of the paper was discussed by the IMF's Executive Board, and the current version has benefited from comments made on that occasion. The opinions expressed in the paper are those of the authors, however, and do not necessarily reflect the views of the IMF or of its Executive Directors.

I   Overview

In 2001–02, Argentina experienced one of the worst economic crises in its history. Output fell by about 20 percent over three years, inflation reignited, the government defaulted on its debt, the banking system was largely paralyzed, and the Argentine peso, which used to be pegged at par with the U.S. dollar, reached lows of 3.90 pesos per U.S. dollar (in June 2002). In the early months of 2003, the economy began to recover, but there remained a long road back to sustained growth and stability.

The events of the crisis, which imposed major hardships on the people of Argentina, are all the more troubling in light of the country's strong past performance. Less than five years earlier, Argentina had been widely hailed as a model of successful economic reform: inflation, which had reached hyperinflationary levels during the 1980s, was in the low single digits, output growth was impressive, and the economy had successfully weathered the Tequila crisis of the mid-1990s. Then, in the late 1990s, the country slipped into a depression from which it was unable to extricate itself. To be sure, there was widespread recognition of underlying vulnerabilities of the economy—which, in hindsight, played a crucial role in the subsequent events—as well as important slippages in policy implementation and, later on, missteps in handling the crisis. But Argentina was widely considered a model reformer and was engaged in a succession of IMF-supported programs (some of which were precautionary) through much of the 1990s, when many of the vulnerabilities were building up.[1]

The severity of the crisis, and the fact that it occurred despite Argentina's reasonable performance in a succession of IMF-supported programs, make it a particularly important case study for other countries and for the IMF. The Argentine experience holds lessons for crisis prevention, crisis management, and the design of IMF-supported programs.[2] This paper examines the origins of the Argentine crisis and its evolution up until early 2002, with a view to drawing out such lessons, some of which have already been reflected in the IMF's work. It focuses on the economic forces leading up to the crisis and the general policy lessons, both for countries' efforts to prevent crises and for the IMF's surveillance and use of its resources.

Like other financial crises in emerging markets during the past decade, the Argentine crisis stemmed from a combination of fragility in balance sheets and the inability to mount an effective policy response.[3] In Argentina, the critical fragility was in public sector debt dynamics, which were made explosive by the effects of a prolonged economic slump and the difficulties in rolling over debt. The inability to mount a policy response stemmed from a combination of economic constraints and political factors— notably, as in many previous crises, insufficient political support and resolve.

Argentina's latest crisis nevertheless differs in several respects from previous ones, as highlighted in a large and rapidly growing academic literature (Box 1).[4] Unlike many traditional balance-of-payments crises—including those suffered by Argentina in the past—this crisis was not driven by large money-financed deficits and high inflation. On the contrary, the currency board regime precluded direct money financing of fiscal deficits, and in the run-up to the crisis there was significant price deflation. Although the small size of Argentina's financial sector contributed to excessive reliance on foreign financing, the banking system appeared sound and well capital-

---

[1]During the 1990s, there were four IMF arrangements: an arrangement under the Extended Fund Facility approved on 3/31/92; a Stand-By Arrangement approved on 4/12/96; another Extended Arrangement, approved on 2/4/98; and another Stand-By Arrangement, approved on 3/10/00. Stand-By Arrangements are short-term arrangements designed to address temporary balance of payments difficulties, while Extended Arrangements focus on balance of payments difficulties arising from longer-term structural problems.

[2]Lessons for crisis management, in particular, based on the experience in a number of countries during the past 10 years, are drawn in a more comprehensive fashion in Collyns and Kincaid (2003).

[3]Previous crises and their origins are reviewed in Ghosh and others (2002).

[4]While individual commentators differ in their emphasis on various factors, the view presented in the paper overlaps with many of the features stressed by Calvo (2002) and Mussa (2002).

Box 1. The Argentine Crisis: A Brief Review of the Academic Literature

The economic literature on Argentina's crisis has mushroomed over the past few years with opinion fairly evenly divided on the roots of the crisis. Mussa (2002) emphasizes that the crisis was rooted in insufficient fiscal tightening in the middle of the decade when the economy was growing at over 7 percent a year, partly related to the overestimation of potential output growth in Argentina during the 1990s. Hausmann and Velasco (2002) argue that the origins of the crisis lie in the sharp downturn of 1998. At that time, expectations of future export growth declined sharply, leading to higher risk premia and smaller capital inflows. This development led to lower domestic investment, which in turn depressed output and further curtailed creditworthiness and the ability to borrow.

Other authors place much greater emphasis on the exchange rate regime in explaining the crisis. Feldstein (2002) argues that the fixed exchange rate made it impossible to achieve competitiveness by a traditional currency devaluation (in contrast to a variety of countries during the 1990s, including Brazil, Korea, and the United Kingdom). Moreover, the resistance of unions to lower wages prevented the fall in production costs that could have achieved the same real devaluation without

a change in the exchange rate. Consistent with this view, Roubini (2001) and De la Torre, Yeyati, and Schmukler (2002) have argued that convertibility does not immunize a country from the balance-sheet effects of a real exchange rate adjustment; it only generates the adjustment through deflation and unemployment, which erodes the repayment capacity of debtors whose earnings come from the nontradable sector. Perry and Serven (2002) also emphasize the existence of a hard peg as a crucial factor in the deteriorating situation. They compare the output adjustment to a terms of trade shock in countries with floating exchange rates and in countries with hard pegs and find that the output adjustment is much greater in the latter, since deflation has to play a large part in the adjustment.

Calvo (2002) emphasizes the sudden reversal of capital flows to Latin America in late 1998 and distinguishes the ability of various Latin American countries to cope with the reversal depending on the degree of openness of the country and the extent of liability dollarization. He argues that since Argentina was a closed economy with an extremely high level of liability dollarization, the change in the real exchange rate required to eliminate the current account deficit was very large.

---

ized (that is, in terms of traditional measures) until the default on government bonds and the asymmetric *pesoization* and *indexation* of bank balance sheets. As with the collapse of Brazil's exchange rate peg in 1999, the public debt dynamics and doubts about the exchange rate peg were central, although the nature of the peg, the timing of exit, and other aspects of the situation led to very different results in the two cases.

In a nutshell, even though the interaction between fiscal policy and the currency board arrangement played the central role in Argentina's transformation from an apparent star performer to a crisis country, a combination of other factors, including unfavorable external developments, was also at play. The currency board, although it initially played an essential role in achieving disinflation, was an inherently risky enterprise; it changed over time from a confidence-enhancer to a confidence-damager, as the policy orientation shifted from a "money-dominant" to a "fiscal-dominant" regime. Once inflation had stabilized at low levels, the rationale for maintaining a fixed exchange rate was weak, given the economy's structural characteristics. Finally, when the economy slid into recession, the currency board became a liability in the context of a buildup of sizable foreign-currency-denominated public debt—signifying the effective fiscal dominance of the policy regime. Not only was the government constrained to carry out a

contractionary monetary policy in the midst of a slump, balance-sheet vulnerabilities had dramatically raised the cost of exiting the fixed exchange-rate regime. The result was a policy dilemma that ultimately undermined the confidence needed to prevent the ensuing crisis.

The paper reviews the four main phases of economic developments and policy responses that led to Argentina's recent crisis. Section II discusses the major vulnerabilities underlying the crisis that emerged during the boom years of the 1990s—in particular, the buildup of public debt and the failure to tackle serious structural weaknesses in fiscal institutions, labor markets, and external trade. Section III describes how these vulnerabilities came into play with the onset of a prolonged depression beginning in mid-1998. Several factors contributed to the downturn, which began as a cyclical correction: domestic political uncertainties, financial contagion from the 1998 Russian crisis, and Brazil's 1999 crisis and the subsequent devaluation of its currency. Once the downturn had started, the currency board arrangement limited the Argentine authorities' ability to prevent a tightening of monetary policy, and the public debt dynamics, which were exacerbated by the protracted slump, ruled out loosening fiscal policy. As a result, the authorities' ability to support economic activity was limited. Section IV takes up events during 2001, as the crisis unfolded in slow motion with a series of increasingly desperate, and in many cases counterproductive, steps to arrest the debt dynamics. Section V discusses the steps taken by the authorities in 2002, following the default on government debt and collapse of the currency board, many of which made the crisis even more difficult to resolve. Section VI examines the IMF's involvement in the unfolding of Argentina's crisis, and Section VII draws out the lessons from Argentina's experience and presents concluding remarks.

II   Boom Years and Buildup of Vulnerabilities: 1992–98

Argentina's 1991 Convertibility Plan seemed to herald a new era of high growth and low inflation, to be founded on disciplined macroeconomic policies and market-oriented structural reform. Real GDP growth, which, on average, had been negative during the 1980s (falling by about ½ percent per year), rebounded sharply to more than 10 percent during the first two years of the stabilization program and more than 5 percent during 1993–94 (Figure 1). After reaching hyperinflationary levels in the late 1980s, inflation fell to single digits by 1993. Capital inflows also began to surge, reflecting newfound confidence in the economy, until the 1995 Tequila crisis interrupted this impressive macroeconomic performance through a sharp reversal of capital flows and a slump in economic activity. However, when Argentina's monetary conditions eased considerably soon after the crisis, and growth rebounded rapidly to 5 percent in 1996 and 8 percent in 1997, many observers only felt the robustness of Argentina's economy confirmed.

Yet underlying this performance were both existing weaknesses and growing vulnerabilities, particularly in the fiscal area, the external and financial sectors, and the labor market. Fiscal performance, while not conspicuously profligate in terms of headline deficit measures, was repeatedly undermined by off-budget expenditures and was too weak throughout the 1990s to prevent a growing reliance on private capital flows to meet the public sector's steadily rising borrowing needs. Exports, though growing at a solid 8 percent per year between 1990 and 1998, did not keep pace with sharply rising import demand, which grew at an average rate of 25 percent per year over the same period. The relatively small domestic financial sector fostered dependence on foreign debt-creating flows to finance both private and public spending. Finally, despite a good start on structural reforms, by mid-decade these were petering out and were, in some cases, even reversed, leaving important rigidities.

These vulnerabilities took on particular importance in the context of Argentina's exchange rate regime. While the currency board brought significant benefits, ending decades of high or hyperinflation, it also implied restrictions on the use of monetary policy and the exchange rate as an adjustment tool, putting much of the onus of macroeconomic stabilization on fiscal policy, and requiring greater nominal flexibility of the economy, especially in the labor market, to absorb external shocks. The logic of a currency board is that the institutional and economic costs of abandoning the regime lend credibility to the peg. But this also means that in cases where persistent external and/or public sector deficits have resulted in the buildup of large exposures, a country is trapped in a regime that, by design, constrains the policy choices available to the authorities. At the time of the introduction of the currency board, IMF staff in its analyses expressed misgivings about the viability of the regime in light of concerns about price and wage competitiveness and the conduct of fiscal policy. Over time, despite the vulnerabilities exposed during the Tequila crisis, the IMF staff's assessment of the currency board regime became more positive.

Public Finances

Despite a booming economy, Argentina's public finances deteriorated during the 1990s (Table 1). The deterioration was the result of moderate headline deficits, averaging some 1½ percent of GDP over 1992–98, combined with persistent off-budget spending. The latter consisted mainly of court-ordered compensation payments after the social security reform of the early 1990s and arrears to suppliers, and raised average new borrowing requirements above 3 percent of GDP per year over this period. While off-budget expenditures tapered off over time, on-balance primary spending grew strongly, accompanied by rising interest payments. As a result, and with the revenue ratio broadly stable, Argentina's estimated structural fiscal position deteriorated from approximate balance in 1992 and 1993 to a deficit of 2¾ percent of GDP by 1998.[5] While it was not obvi-

---

[5]The calculations of the structural balance are sensitive to assumptions about potential output growth, which are inherently uncertain. While Table 1 assumes potential growth of close to 3½ percent during this period, the estimated cumulative structural deterioration would be higher (lower) by about 1¼ percentage point, if potential growth was assumed to be 1 percentage point lower (higher).

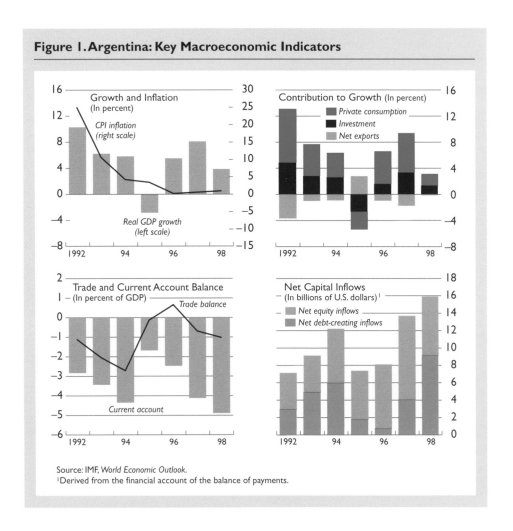

Figure 1. Argentina: Key Macroeconomic Indicators

Source: IMF, *World Economic Outlook*.
[1]Derived from the financial account of the balance of payments.

ous that deficits of this magnitude were a problem, provided that growth rates remained at 5 percent or above, they spelled vulnerability in the event of much slower growth. This was the case because Argentina, instead of building up fiscal cushions during the boom period, had accumulated considerable amounts of new debt.

Spending—both on- and off-budget—was the main driving force behind the deteriorating public debt dynamics during this period. The federal government's off-budget expenditures explain nearly 9 percentage points of the 10 percentage point increase in the public debt ratio from 31 percent of GDP in 1992 to 41 percent in 1998 (Table 2).[6] Capitalized interest and valuation changes were roughly offset by privatization receipts, and both the primary deficit (excluding off-budget activities) as well as the endogenous debt dynamics—arising from the differ-

ential between growth and interest rates—had a roughly neutral impact on the debt ratio. This does not mean that budgetary performance was prudent, though: real primary spending (deflated by the GDP deflator) was allowed to grow by a cumulative 35 percent, or 5½ percent a year, during 1993–98.

A more cautious fiscal stance during this period could have greatly improved the public debt dynamics and likely prevented Argentina's eventual default. This can be illustrated by contrasting the actual debt dynamics with a hypothetical alternative fiscal scenario. For example, if real on-budget spending increases had been limited to 3 percent a year, given the estimated average growth rate of potential GDP during the 1993–2001 period, the public debt ratio would have decreased to 26½ percent of GDP in 1998 even with unchanged off-budget activities (Table 2, bottom panel). Moreover, such a policy would have kept the debt ratio below 35 percent in 2001 (under the realized path of interest rates and GDP growth), thereby greatly reducing the government's borrowing needs.

---

[6]From 1996 on, off-budget transactions by the provinces added another estimated 0.2 to 0.4 percentage points of GDP annually to the public debt ratio.

Table 1. Fiscal Indicators
(In percent of GDP, unless otherwise indicated)

	1992	1993	1994	1995	1996	1997	1998	1999	2000	2001
Overall public sector[1]										
Balance (excluding										
capitalized interest)	–0.4	0.0	–1.4	–2.3	–3.1	–2.0	–2.0	–4.1	–3.6	–6.3
Revenue	23.4	24.6	24.2	23.2	22.2	23.2	23.8	24.3	24.7	23.6
Expenditure	23.8	24.6	25.6	25.5	25.4	25.3	25.9	28.5	28.4	29.9
Primary balance	1.4	1.4	0.2	–0.5	–1.1	0.3	0.6	–0.7	0.4	–1.4
Structural balance[2]	0.0	0.0	–2.0	–1.4	–2.7	–2.6	–2.8	–3.5	–2.1	–3.1
Fiscal impulse[3]	...	0.5	1.8	–0.8	1.1	–0.2	–0.1	–0.2	–1.9	0.1
Revenue impulse	...	–1.1	0.3	1.0	1.0	–1.0	–0.6	–0.5	–0.4	1.2
Expenditure impulse	...	1.5	1.4	–1.9	0.1	0.6	0.5	0.4	–1.5	–1.1
Debt (end of period)	30.7	30.6	33.7	36.7	39.1	37.7	40.9	47.6	50.9	62.2
Interest expenditure in										
percent of revenue	8.1	5.8	6.4	8.0	9.3	10.1	11.0	14.0	16.4	20.6
Inclusion of off-budget										
federal expenditure[4]										
Balance	–3.1	–3.4	–3.9	–3.4	–4.0	–2.6	–2.5	–4.8	–4.2	–6.9
Primary balance	–1.2	–2.0	–2.4	–1.5	–1.9	–0.3	0.2	–1.4	–0.1	–2.0
Structural balance	–2.6	–3.5	–4.5	–2.5	–3.6	–3.2	–3.2	–4.1	–2.7	–3.6
Impulse[3]	...	1.3	0.9	–2.4	1.0	–0.5	–0.2	0.1	–2.1	0.1
Federal government										
Balance	–0.2	0.9	–0.5	–0.9	–2.5	–1.6	–1.3	–2.5	–2.5	–4.4
Revenue	19.0	19.9	19.4	18.6	17.6	18.5	19.0	19.4	19.6	18.8
Expenditure	19.2	19.0	19.9	19.6	20.1	20.1	20.3	21.9	22.1	23.2
Primary balance	1.5	2.1	0.8	0.6	–0.8	0.4	0.9	0.4	0.9	0.1
Structural balance[2,5]	0.0	0.9	–0.8	–0.4	–2.3	–1.9	–1.7	–2.2	–1.6	–2.7
Fiscal impulse[3,5]	...	–0.5	1.5	–0.6	1.7	–0.5	–0.5	–0.2	–1.0	0.0
Provincial governments										
Balance	–0.2	–0.9	–0.9	–1.4	–0.6	–0.5	–0.8	–1.6	–1.2	–1.9
Fiscal impulse[3,5]	...	1.0	0.3	–0.2	–0.6	0.3	0.4	0.1	–0.9	0.2
Memorandum items:										
Growth of real GDP										
(in percent)	10.3	5.7	5.8	–2.8	5.5	8.1	3.9	–3.4	–0.8	–4.5
Growth of potential GDP										
(in percent)[6]	3.5	3.5	3.5	3.4	3.5	3.5	3.0	2.6	2.4	2.4
Output gap (in percent of										
potential GDP) [7]	–2.1	0.1	2.4	–3.8	–1.9	2.5	3.3	–2.7	–5.7	–12.1
Off-budget expenditure of										
federal government[4]	2.7	3.4	2.5	1.0	0.9	0.5	0.4	0.7	0.6	0.6

[1] Consolidated fiscal accounts of federal and provincial governments.

[2] Actual balance corrected for the economic cycle (i.e., the difference between actual and potential GDP).

[3] The impulse identifies the changes in the fiscal balance that are not due to cyclical fluctuations or changes in interest payments. A positive impulse defines an expansionary policy stance.

[4] Includes various court-ordered compensation payments, including to pensioners and former victims of political prosecution.

[5] For the purpose of deriving the structural balance and the fiscal impulse by the two subsectors of government, revenue and expenditure of the federal government are adjusted to exclude transfers to provinces.

[6] Derived on the basis of a Hodrick-Prescott filter using quarterly GDP data from 1995 onward.

[7] Positive figure indicates GDP above potential.

Table 2. Public Sector Debt Dynamics

(In percent of GDP, unless otherwise indicated)

	1992	1993	1994	1995	1996	1997	1998	1999	2000	2001
					Actual Developments					
Public sector debt	**30.7**	**30.6**	**33.7**	**36.7**	**39.1**	**37.7**	**40.9**	**47.6**	**50.9**	**62.2**
Of which: foreign-currency denominated	27.8	27.7	30.6	33.3	35.4	34.2	38.0	44.2	48.7	60.7
Change in public sector debt	...	−0.1	3.2	3.0	2.4	−1.4	3.2	6.8	3.3	11.3
Primary deficit	...	−1.4	−0.2	0.5	1.1	−0.3	−0.6	0.7	−0.4	1.4
Revenue and grants	...	24.6	24.2	23.2	22.2	23.2	23.8	24.3	24.7	23.6
Primary (noninterest) expenditure	...	23.2	24.1	23.7	23.3	22.9	23.2	25.1	24.3	25.0
Endogenous debt dynamics[1]	...	−1.8	−0.9	1.8	0.2	−0.4	1.9	5.6	3.9	7.8
Other net debt-creating flows	...	3.2	4.3	0.7	1.1	−0.6	1.9	0.4	−0.2	2.1
Privatization receipts (negative)	...	−0.4	−0.4	−0.6	−0.4	−0.6	−0.2	−1.0	−0.1	−0.1
Off-budget federal government expenditure	...	3.4	2.5	1.1	0.9	0.5	0.4	0.7	0.6	0.6
Other[2]	...	0.1	2.1	0.3	0.7	−0.6	1.7	0.7	−0.7	1.6
Public sector debt in percent of revenues	...	124.3	139.1	157.9	175.8	162.5	171.6	195.7	205.8	263.9
Gross financing need of federal government[3]	...	...	...	4.4	5.5	5.9	7.0	9.2	9.3	13.8
in billions of U.S. dollars	...	...	...	11.4	15.1	17.2	20.9	26.1	26.6	37.0
Key macroeconomic and fiscal variables										
Real GDP growth (in percent)	...	5.7	5.8	−2.8	5.5	8.1	3.9	−3.4	−0.8	−4.4
Nominal effective interest rate on public debt (in percent)[4]	...	5.3	5.6	5.5	5.9	6.4	7.1	7.9	8.5	9.0
Real effective interest rate (in percent)[5]	...	−1.6	2.7	2.4	6.0	6.9	8.8	9.7	7.5	10.1
Inflation rate (GDP deflator, in percent)	...	6.9	2.8	3.2	−0.1	−0.5	−1.7	−1.8	1.0	−1.1
Growth of real primary spending (in percent)	...	11.6	9.9	−4.4	3.8	6.3	5.3	4.2	−3.8	−1.6
				Alternative Scenario: 3 Percent Annual Growth in Real Primary Spending						
Public sector debt	**30.7**	**28.8**	**28.7**	**29.8**	**30.4**	**26.7**	**26.5**	**27.9**	**27.8**	**34.8**
Change in public sector debt	...	−1.9	0.0	1.1	0.6	−3.7	−0.3	1.4	−0.1	7.0
Primary deficit	...	−3.2	−3.4	−1.2	−0.7	−2.7	−3.5	−2.6	−2.2	0.7
Revenue and grants	...	24.6	24.2	23.2	22.2	23.2	23.8	24.3	24.7	23.6
Primary (noninterest) expenditure	...	21.4	20.8	22.1	21.5	20.5	20.4	21.7	22.5	24.3
Endogenous debt dynamics[1,6]	...	−1.8	−0.9	1.5	0.1	−0.3	1.3	3.6	2.3	4.3
Other net debt-creating flows	...	3.2	4.3	0.7	1.1	−0.6	1.9	0.4	−0.2	2.1
Overall public sector balance[6]	−0.4	1.8	2.0	−0.4	−1.0	0.9	1.6	0.4	−0.2	−3.4
Gross financing need of federal government[3,7]	...	...	...	2.1	2.9	2.0	1.8	2.7	3.4	7.5
in billions of U.S. dollars	...	...	...	5.5	7.9	5.8	5.2	7.7	9.8	20.2

[1] Endogenous debt dynamics result from the interest rate/growth differential and are derived as $[(i − \pi) − g\,(1+\pi)]/(1+g+\pi+g\pi)$ times previous period debt ratio, with i = nominal effective interest rate; π = growth rate of GDP deflator; and g = real GDP growth rate.

[2] Including valuation changes, capitalized interest, and other debt-creating transactions of provincial governments which added an estimated 0.2 to 0.4 percent of GDP annually to the public debt ratio during 1996–2001.

[3] Defined as fiscal deficit, plus amortization of medium- and long-term debt, plus short-term debt at end of previous period. The federal government has accounted for about 90 percent of public debt over this period.

[4] Derived as nominal interest expenditure divided by previous period debt stock.

[5] Nominal rate minus change in GDP deflator.

[6] Assumes that the effective interest rate on public debt remains unchanged.

[7] Assumes unchanged average maturity of medium- and long-term debt and unchanged share of short-term in total debt.

Perhaps the most serious misperception underlying policy errors during this period was an overly optimistic view of Argentina's growth potential. Strong growth performance following the macroeconomic stabilization in the early 1990s, together with structural reforms and low inflation, led most observers—in the IMF, as well as in academia and private markets—to believe that Argentina's potential growth had increased permanently to as much as 5 percent per year.[7] This conclusion seemed to be supported by a rise in labor productivity.[8] The economy's resilience during the Tequila crisis also seemed to confirm that Argentina had entered an era of noninflationary high growth.

In hindsight, the expansion of Argentina's economy during the 1990s appears to have reflected, in large part, a number of temporary factors. In particular, the high growth of the early 1990s may have reflected the low starting point associated with the adverse economic effects of the hyperinflation of the 1980s. In addition, private consumption—the main contributor to growth during this period—was fueled by a surge of durables consumption that, in turn, spurred private investment. Given the nature of this stock adjustment, once consumers had upgraded their possession of durables, consumption, investment, and growth would tend to return to more normal levels.[9] Indeed, recent empirical estimates suggest that Argentina's potential growth rate was closer to 3 to $3\frac{1}{2}$ percent during this period and lower in 1999–2001 (see Appendix I). Moreover, while the Tequila episode demonstrated the resilience of the economy, it also showed that Argentina's growth rate remained highly volatile.[10] In particular, the crisis demonstrated the tendency for a currency board to bring about a procyclical monetary contraction in response to market pressures; and while Argentina navigated the crisis successfully during the Tequila crisis, the authorities began to deviate from the rigid rules of the currency board—for instance, by engaging in swaps and repurchase agreements to limit the

automatic monetary contraction. The skill of the policymakers in facing these pressures made the regime seem more robust than it actually was.

The optimism regarding the country's growth potential deflected attention from the underlying public debt dynamics. With average effective interest rates of 5 to 6 percent per year, moderately positive inflation rates, and assumed potential real growth of 5 percent, the autonomous debt dynamics appeared benign, fostering complacency about the growing indebtedness. The strength of the growth prospects seemed, at the time, to justify the rapid expansion of real primary spending that took place.

The rising debt ratio, however, generated steadily growing financing needs and vulnerability to adverse shifts in market conditions. As a result of the government's on- and off-budget activities, as well as the graduated repayment schedule of the 1993 Brady rescheduling—which had brought welcome breathing space during earlier years—the federal government's gross financing needs nearly doubled in the four years to 1998 to $20 billion or about 25 percent of total private emerging market bond financing. This ratio would rise to more than one-third in 2000–01. Thus, even with adept debt management, evidenced by relatively long average maturities and limited reliance on short-term debt or floating rate instruments, rollover risks rose sharply.[11] This left the public finances vulnerable to a shift in market sentiment and to a downturn in economic growth—both of which began to transpire in the second half of 1998.

The room for fiscal maneuver was further reduced by decentralization and structural weaknesses on both the expenditure and the revenue sides. The extensive decentralization of responsibility for public expenditure, combined with an overly complex intergovernmental transfer system and the provinces' ability to borrow, impeded effective countercyclical policies in the years of high growth and a more forceful response to the rising fiscal pressures in the later years (Box 2). Moreover, with transfers to provinces absorbing some 30 percent of the federal government budget, and, by 1998, social security benefits swallowing another 30 percent, and interest payments another 10 percent, the federal government's scope for short-term fiscal adjustment was severely constrained. At the same time, revenue performance displayed considerable weakness. Although by 1998 the revenue ratio, at some 24 percent of GDP, had broadly recovered from the effects of the

---

[7]IMF staff's medium-term scenario in early 1998, for example, explicitly assumed a potential output growth rate of 5 percent.

[8]Labor productivity (measured as GDP per employed worker) grew by nearly 3 percent per year over the period 1990–98; this, combined with a steady growth in the working-age population of about 2 percent per year, yields the 5 percent growth of potential output.

[9]This pattern is consistent with theoretical models of exchange-rate based stabilizations. The rapid decline in inflation associated with such a stabilization generates a wealth effect that induces consumers to bring forward their purchases of durable goods. Once this stock adjustment has taken place, demand for durables declines until the next replacement cycle.

[10]The standard deviation of Argentina's growth rate fell only slightly from $4\frac{1}{2}$ percent in 1980–90 to $4\frac{1}{4}$ percent in 1991–98. This compares with a decline from 5 percent to $2\frac{1}{4}$ percent in Brazil and from $6\frac{3}{4}$ percent to $2\frac{3}{4}$ percent in Chile over the same period.

[11]The average maturity of the government's medium- and long-term debt (measured as the ratio of total debt to annual amortization payments) exceeded 10 years even in 1999–2000 (compared with about six years for the United States) and was considerably higher in the mid-1990s, while short-term debt was less than 5 percent of total debt (30 percent in the United States).

Box 2. Argentina's Intergovernmental Relations[1]

Argentina's constitution provides for a significant degree of decentralization of public expenditure responsibilities. Spending by provincial governments, which carry the main responsibility for health and education, hovered at around 11 percent of GDP through the 1990s—some 45 percent of total public sector spending. Revenue generation, in contrast, has been dominated by federal taxes, with provincial governments traditionally collecting less than 4 percent of GDP in tax revenues, largely from their own turnover and property taxes. This imbalance has given rise to a complex system of transfers that has channeled some 6 percent of GDP per year from the federal government to the provinces. In addition, provinces have enjoyed considerable latitude in borrowing, because they are legally able to pledge their income from future transfers as collateral to creditors

This fiscal federal structure gave rise to a number of problems, some of which are common also to other federal systems (the United States, Germany, Switzerland):

- *The spending autonomy of the provinces, combined with their ability to borrow, obstructed efforts to consolidate the public finances.* In 1997–99, in particular, when the federal government tightened policies by a cumulative equivalent of 1¼ percentage points of GDP to offset part of the cyclical deterioration, the provinces loosened their policy stance by

¾ percentage point of GDP. During this period, their already bloated payroll (with wage rates often exceeding their private sector equivalent) rose by over 1 percentage point of GDP alongside a surge in public sector employment.

- *The intergovernmental transfer system became overly complex,* with different sharing arrangements for different taxes. Frequent adjustment of rules encouraged provinces to press for higher transfers while creating incentives for the federal government to introduce distortive taxes that were not shared (such as the financial transactions tax, initially, and the export tax). As such, the system became a major source of inefficiency and tension in fiscal policy.

- *Provinces had little incentive to improve their own revenue performance* in the presence of growing co-participated and discretionary transfers. Indeed, only a small fraction of their rising expenditure was covered by increases in provincial taxes.

- *The revenue-sharing arrangement led to procyclical provincial policies.* Particularly in years of fast growth when the economy was operating above its estimated potential (such as 1994 and 1997–98), the provinces added stimulus. Ironically, a temporary replacement of the procyclical system by a flat monthly transfer—negotiated in late 2000 to allow the federal budget to reap the benefits from a new tax package—became effectively a floor on transfers to the provinces in 2001 when revenues fell below their expected level.

---

[1] For a more in-depth discussion of intergovernmental fiscal relations in Argentina, see Cuevas (2003).

---

earlier pension reform,[12] it remained low in comparison with many other emerging market countries—though not necessarily with countries in the region (Figure 2). More important, as evidenced by a comparison of tax efficiency across countries, the low revenue ratio in Argentina was not so much a reflection of favorable tax rates as of missed opportunities during the 1990s to strengthen the tax base and to curb widespread evasion.[13] The narrowness of the

tax base and weaknesses in tax administration left limited scope for raising revenues when the budgetary situation later deteriorated.

Underlying the problems in the public finances were deep-rooted social and political tensions. Up until the early 1990s, Argentina had often resolved such tensions with periodic bouts of high inflation. Since the currency board regime ruled out inflationary finance, and the tensions were not tackled directly, competing claims on economic resources by various social groups ended up being reconciled by rising public sector indebtedness.[14] Although Argentina compares fairly well with many other Latin American countries in terms of institutional strength, the widespread perception of corruption—which appears to have risen during the late 1990s while remaining fairly stable in Chile and Mexico and falling considerably in Brazil (Table 3)—only added to the socio-political divisions that made it impossible to

---

[12]The pension reform, introducing a funded pillar, served to reduce future government liabilities, but implied revenue losses in the transition period of an estimated 1 to 2 percent of GDP a year.

[13]The comparison in Figure 2 is based on value added tax (VAT) revenue only. A comparison of the productivity of personal and corporate income taxes is hampered by different tax brackets and limited data availability. Nevertheless, a rough measure (using average and top rates) for a subgroup of countries confirms Argentina's comparatively weak revenue collection. Symptomatic, also, are the costs of tax collection, which were about 2 to 2½ percent of revenues in Argentina, compared with about 1½ percent in Brazil and Mexico, ½ percent in Chile, and less than ½ percent in the United States.

[14]This argument is forcefully made in Hirschman (1985).

Figure 2. Revenue Performance in Selected Emerging Market Countries, Averages 1996–2000[1]

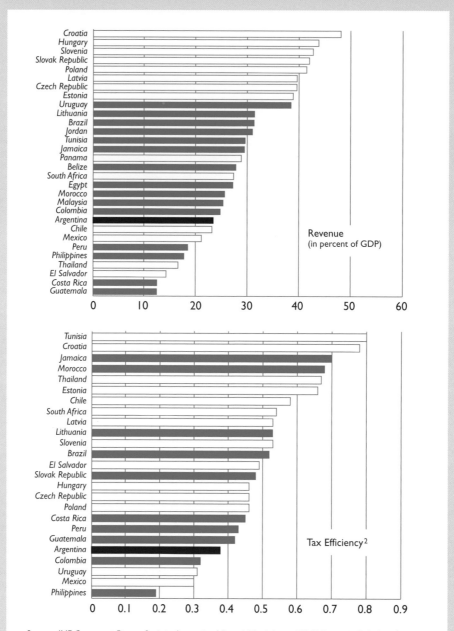

Sources: IMF, *Government Finance Statistics, International Financial Statistics, and World Economic Outlook*; and Corporate Taxes 2001–2002, Worldwide Summaries (PricewaterhouseCoopers).

[1]Includes all countries with investment or speculative grade ratings by Moody's, Standard and Poor's or both, as of January 2001, plus Brazil. White bars indicate countries with investment grade rating by at least one of the two rating agencies.

[2]Derived as value added tax (VAT) revenue in percent of consumption, divided by standard VAT rate.

Table 3. Ratings of Institutional Strength and Corruption
(scaled from 0 to 10)

	Institutional Strength[1]		Corruption[2]	
	1995	2001	1995	2001
Latin American countries				
Chile	6.7	7.3	7.9	7.5
Argentina	6.7	7.2	5.2	3.5
Mexico	5.8	6.8	3.2	3.7
Brazil	5.6	5.0	2.7	4.0
OECD countries				
Canada	10.0	10.0	8.9	8.9
Sweden	10.0	10.0	8.9	9.0
Australia	9.6	9.6	8.8	8.5
France	9.2	7.5	7.0	6.7
Italy	7.4	7.1	3.0	5.5
Other emerging markets				
India	6.9	7.0	2.8	2.7
Philippines	5.2	5.6	2.8	2.9
Malaysia	6.7	5.1	5.3	5.0
South Africa	7.9	5.0	5.6	4.8
Indonesia	5.7	4.4	1.9	1.9

Sources: International Country Risk Guide, Political Risk Services Group; Transparency International.

[1] The rating is the average of the ratings for "law and order," "freedom from corruption," "democratic accountability" and "bureaucratic quality." For each of these categories, higher numbers indicate that institutions are better.

[2] The index is scaled on the degree of cleanliness so that 0 is the most corrupt and 10 is the most clean.

garner the necessary support for decisive adjustment when it was needed.[15]

The Structural Setting

External Sector

The export sector's limited contribution to the economy—accounting for around 10 percent of GDP—was a key weakness of the Argentine economy. First, it limited the ability of the external sector to provide a buffer against swings in domestic demand. When private consumption and investment went into a sharp downturn in mid-1998, the economy could not plausibly export its way out of recession. Second, it made the economy more vulnerable to shifts of investor sentiment in international capital markets. When capital flows were curtailed, the ability to generate export revenues to pay for imports and debt service was limited—a particular concern for international liquidity given that, under the cur-

rency board regime, international reserves were needed to back the domestic currency. Third, even with a relatively moderate external debt-to-GDP ratio of less than 50 percent in 1998 (of which about three-fifths was public sector), the low export share implied a precariously high debt-to-export ratio of 455 percent, with debt-service payments alone absorbing three-quarters of annual export earnings (Figure 3). This made external sustainability highly susceptible to any slowdown in export growth. Moreover, to the extent that the real exchange rate was overvalued, the debt-to-GDP ratio was misleadingly low. Through late 1998, exports were projected by IMF staff to grow at about 12 percent in 1999 and the debt-to-export ratio was projected to stabilize at 450 percent. In the event, export revenues declined by more than 12 percent and the debt-to-export ratio rose to 530 percent, bringing debt sustainability increasingly into question.

One of the factors behind the low export share was the sharp appreciation of the real exchange rate during the early stages of stabilization. Between 1991 and 1993, the CPI-based real effective exchange rate appreciated by almost 25 percent. Although exports grew rapidly during this period, they did so from a very low base, and the real appreciation may have

---

[15]It should be noted, however, that the perception of corruption is correlated with the economic situation: Argentina's deteriorating corruption index (at least after 1998) may thus, in part, also reflect the deepening crisis.

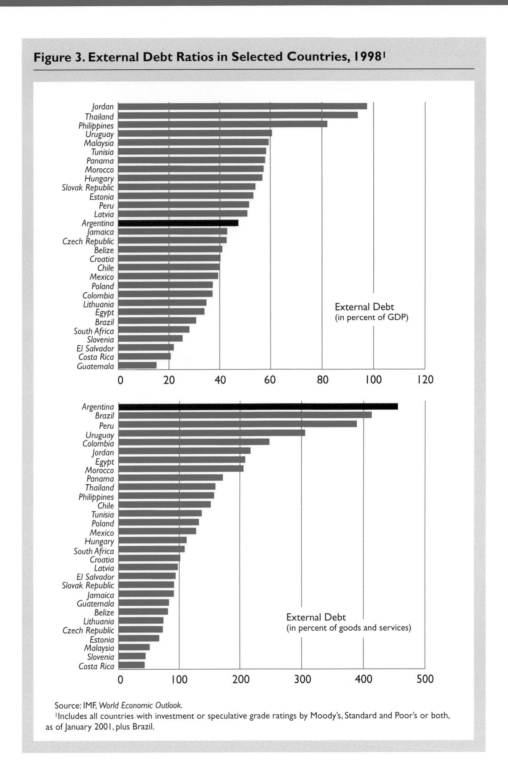

Figure 3. External Debt Ratios in Selected Countries, 1998[1]

Source: IMF, *World Economic Outlook*.
[1]Includes all countries with investment or speculative grade ratings by Moody's, Standard and Poor's or both, as of January 2001, plus Brazil.

impeded further export expansion and diversification (although this impact was partly offset by a lowering of export taxes in 2002, from about 4 percent of the value of exports to close to zero). While it is impossible to prove that Argentina's exports would have

performed much better under a flexible exchange rate arrangement once trade was liberalized, it is striking that other countries that have undergone major trade liberalizations and were considerably more successful in boosting export shares (such as

Spain in the mid-1970s, Chile during the 1970s and 1980s, and Turkey in the early 1980s) have done so in the context of a depreciating real exchange rate (Box 3). From 1993 until 1998, Argentina's CPI-based competitiveness remained roughly unchanged (Figure 4), while the (less reliable) unit labor cost measure of the real effective exchange rate depreciated by about 30 percent. However, the latter is based on industrial sector wages only, representing a relatively small share of Argentina's export sector. Moreover, both exchange rate measures fail to capture the "true" competitiveness of Argentine products, to the extent that Mercosur implicitly sheltered the regional market from foreign competition in higher quality goods (see below).

Indeed, the concentration of Argentina's exports in primary products and to Mercosur (Brazil, in particular) represented a major vulnerability. About 20 percent of Argentina's exports are primary prod-

ucts (and a further 35 percent closely related agricultural manufactures) that are subject to substantial trade barriers, low price elasticities, and wide swings in prices. Between mid-1996 and mid-1998, for example, the world price of Argentina's commodity exports fell by 25 percent, followed by a further 20 percent decline in 1998 (Figure 5). Argentina's exports also became highly concentrated geographically during the 1990s, partly as a result of trade diversion toward the Mercosur region, as exports to other markets grew much more slowly. Mercosur was established in 1991, removing tariffs between Argentina, Brazil, Paraguay, and Uruguay, and was followed by a free trade agreement with Chile and Bolivia. In 1991, Mercosur plus Chile and Bolivia accounted for 20 percent of Argentina's exports; by 1998, that proportion had risen to 45 percent, with Brazil making up two-thirds of this. In addition,

---

Box 3. Trade Liberalization and Real Exchange Rate Dynamics—Evidence from Other Countries

One of the main factors contributing to a rapid rise in Argentina's debt-to-export ratio during the 1990s was an inability to substantially increase the country's export market share when trade was liberalized. The share of exports in GDP rose only slightly over this period, whereas the behavior of the export ratio in a number of countries that started out at Argentina's level of openness has been much more robust following the liberalization of their trade regimes (see the figure).

In the mid-1970s when **Spain** changed from an autocratic to a democratic regime, the economy became more open, with increased tourist revenue and capital inflows. Moreover, the 20 percent devaluation of the peso in 1977 and the additional devaluation of 8 percent in 1982 helped to maintain the momentum on export growth although rising labor costs partially undermined this price effect (see figure). Over the 10-year period between 1976 and 1985, the ratio of exports to GDP rose by 10 percentage points to 22 percent. Most of the trade gains between the mid-1970s and mid-1980s occurred in mechanical machinery, motor vehicles, petroleum products, and foodstuffs. Since then the economy has continued to transform itself, associated with a program of deregulation and privatization in the mid-1980s (shipbuilding and steel production) and entry into the European Union (in 1986).

In 1973, **Chile's** military government initiated a deep structural reform program with trade liberalization playing a central part. Between 1974 and 1979, the import substitution model was dismantled with all nontariff barriers eliminated in 1976 and a uniform tariff of 10 percent set in 1979. Although the tariff rate rose in the early 1980s associated with the debt crisis, it returned to 11 percent in 1991. Over the 20-year period between 1973 and 1992, the ratio of exports to GDP rose by 30 percentage points to 35 percent, accompanied by considerable product diversification, with the contribution of mining ex-

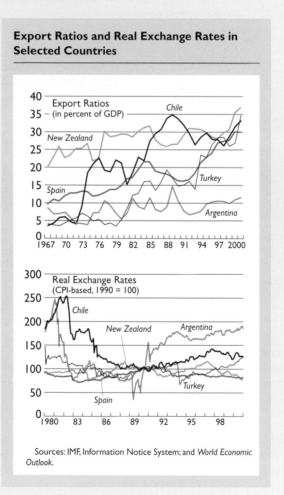

Export Ratios and Real Exchange Rates in Selected Countries

Sources: IMF, Information Notice System; and *World Economic Outlook*.

Box 3 (*concluded*)

ports falling from over 80 percent during 1960–73 to 46 percent over the 1991–99 period. This performance was boosted by a 50 percent real depreciation of the currency between 1980 and 1991, government assistance in improving supply responses by correcting key market failures, and an active effort to gather information on foreign markets.

New Zealand's economy is similar to the Argentine economy in many ways, especially in its concentration of natural resource intensive exports. In the early 1970s, natural resources (meat, wool, and dairy) accounted for over 90 percent of New Zealand's exports, most of which went to the United Kingdom. However, in 1973, when the United Kingdom joined the European Union, New Zealand's preferential market access vanished and it had to adjust to tougher competition in this market. Historically, New Zealand's trade regime was dominated by import licenses, which only began to get rolled back in 1979. In 1984, the new government initiated a move to replace licenses with tariffs by selling import licenses to the highest bidder. This policy eventually led to a decline in the tariff rate to 7 percent by 1996–97 (broadly at the level of other OECD countries) from 28 percent in the mid-1980s. At the time of the introduction of the tariffication process the authorities also floated the currency but these policies had little impact on the export ratio over the 1975–95 period, which stayed fairly constant at 30 percent, as the real exchange

rate did not vary much over this period. Between 1995 and 2001, however, the export ratio rose by 7 percentage points to 37 percent, while the currency depreciated by 15 percent.

Following a severe exchange rate crisis in the late 1970s, **Turkey** undertook a structural adjustment program with the objective of transforming its economy from import substitution to export orientation. This objective was to be achieved through real exchange rate depreciation, export subsidies, and import liberalization. Over the period 1981–91 the real exchange rate depreciated by about 20 percent, facilitating a sharp rise in exports. During the early 1980s export credits were given at preferential rates of interest, and tax rebates were also offered until 1989. These policies contributed to a rise in the export ratio from 5 percent to 17 percent of GDP by 1989, with the share of manufactures in total exports rising from 36 to 78 percent over the same period.

It appears that the combination of trade liberalization and real exchange rate depreciation contributed to the strong export performance of Chile, Spain, and Turkey during the 1980s whereas the absence of any noticeable real exchange rate movement in New Zealand hindered this adjustment. This finding suggests that Argentina's failure to substantially raise its export share during the 1990s may be associated with the currency board, to the extent that it constrained downward adjustments in the real exchange rate.

---

some studies of trade patterns suggest that the trade diversion toward Mercosur went hand-in-hand with a shift toward uncompetitive capital intensive goods, and industry-level studies have shown that (most notably for automobiles) quality remained lower, and prices higher, than in the world market.[16] The Mercosur trading arrangement may thus have amplified the effect of the peso's real appreciation by contributing to Argentina's low export share as well as its vulnerability to adverse commodity price developments and, increasingly, to weaker regional demand, particularly from Brazil.

Argentina's export performance must also be viewed against the behavior of imports, a major factor contributing to the rise in the external debt ratio during the 1990s. Imports in nominal terms recorded phenomenal growth rates in the early 1990s following Argentina's trade liberalization program in the late 1980s, when the average tariff rate was reduced from 45 percent to around 10 percent. Therefore, although export receipts grew at about 8 percent per year between 1990 and 1998, they did not keep pace with imports, which grew at an average rate of 25

percent per year over the same period, with particularly high growth rates in the first two years following the macroeconomic stabilization. While the real exchange rate appreciation and tariff reductions doubtless contributed to the import boom, an implied high income elasticity of imports meant that economic growth, while tending to reduce the ratio of the existing stock of debt in relation to GDP, also contributed to the further accumulation of debt through a wider trade deficit.

Financial System

Although Argentina's domestic financial system was not at the root of its crisis, it contributed to the buildup of vulnerabilities by encouraging heavy reliance on foreign lending and extensive informal dollarization. Notwithstanding significant financial deepening during the 1990s, the financial system in Argentina remained relatively underdeveloped by wider international comparison—though it was roughly comparable to that of Brazil and Mexico. All three Latin American countries rank low in standard measures of financial development, such as equity market capitalization, total domestic credit, private

---

[16]Yeats (1998); and Chudnovsky, Lopez, and Porta (1996).

Figure 4. Exports, Imports, Terms of Trade, and Real Exchange Rate

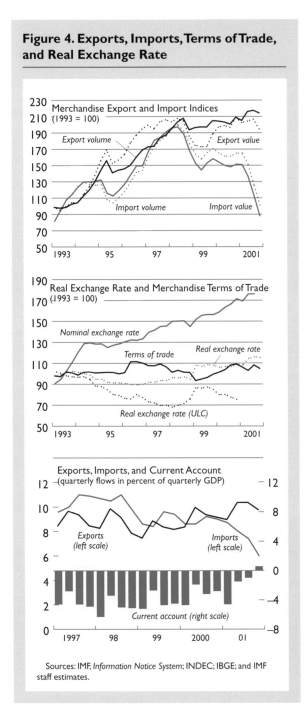

Sources: IMF, *Information Notice System*; INDEC; IBGE; and IMF staff estimates.

Figure 5. Export Performance

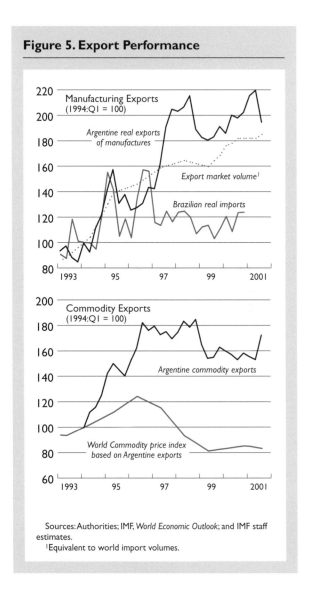

Sources: Authorities; IMF, *World Economic Outlook*; and IMF staff estimates.
[1] Equivalent to world import volumes.

sector credit, and M2—expressed in relation to GDP (Figure 6). Clearly, excessive reliance on the domestic banking sector can also create problems in a crisis, by spreading and magnifying the repercussions of financial shocks to the entire economy (as in Thailand in 1997). But a low level of domestic financial intermediation and little recourse to equity financing, as in Argentina, contributed to excessive reliance on

foreign lending and thus a higher risk of liquidity problems.[17]

Moreover, notwithstanding a significant strengthening of the Argentine banking system in the course of the 1990s, banks were exposed to a number of risks that subsequently materialized. Argentina's financial sector underwent a significant transformation during the 1990s, with banking-system efficiency improving strongly as a result of substantial consolidation, privatization, and increased entry of foreign institutions. The consolidation, which halved the number of institutions, went hand-in-hand with improvements in the regulatory framework and

---

[17]A reason for the lower liquidity risk associated with domestic borrowing is the wider range of collateral, such as real estate, that is acceptable to domestic, but not to foreign, lenders (see Caballero and Krishnamurthy, 2002).

Figure 6. Indicators of Financial Market Development in Selected Countries, Averages 1997–99

(In percent of GDP)

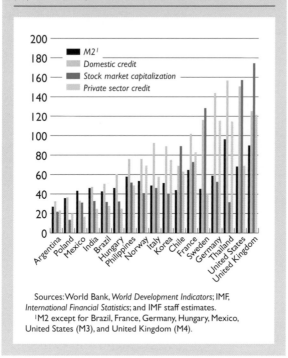

Sources: World Bank, *World Development Indicators*; IMF, *International Financial Statistics*; and IMF staff estimates.

[1]M2 except for Brazil, France, Germany, Hungary, Mexico, United States (M3), and United Kingdom (M4).

strengthened supervision, especially after the Tequila crisis (during which 18 percent of total deposits were withdrawn in the space of three months). Nevertheless, while the banking system that emerged from this transformation was highly liquid and reasonably well capitalized by standard measures, banks' profitability remained relatively low even before the recession, and high dollarization (despite positive net asset positions) exposed institutions to credit risk in the event of a devaluation—as both corporates and households relying on domestic-currency earnings borrowed extensively in dollars—and to liquidity risk in the event of a systemic bank run.[18] Finally, banks' exposure to the public sector grew steadily from about 10 percent of total assets at the end of 1994 to more than 20 percent at the end of 2000. The large and relatively weak public banks in particular—which accounted for one-third of the system's total assets but half of all nonperforming loans at the end of 2000—were highly exposed to the government. While such exposures to government debt

were not captured by standard measures of capital adequacy, they proved critical in the context of the government default that ultimately occurred. Thus, the banking system was vulnerable to three forms of shocks, all of which eventually materialized: economic downturn, devaluation of the exchange rate, and default by the public sector. Foreign-owned banks had contributed to a strengthening of the banking system, because they were less tied to the domestic economy (and politics) and therefore more robust, but their weaker domestic linkages had a downside. Like other international creditors, foreign-owned banks reduced their exposure when financial risks increased.

Labor Market

Like any fixed exchange rate system, the currency board required flexible domestic prices and wages to mitigate the impact of economic shocks on output and employment. Historically, labor regulation in Argentina has been highly protective of individual workers, imposing high barriers to dismissal and guaranteeing generous fringe benefits. In addition, collective bargaining at the industry level greatly reduced wage flexibility. While motivated by a desire for social cohesion and fairness, these protections were an additional element hampering Argentina's ability to cope with exogenous shocks.

During the first half of the 1990s, the government embarked on a number of reforms aimed at enhancing labor market flexibility. These reforms took place in three phases: 1991, 1995, and 1998. The first set of reforms in 1991 represented a modest improvement in labor market flexibility, introducing fixed-term contracts and special training contracts for young workers. In 1995, the government, business organizations, and the Confederation of Labor reached agreement on facilitating temporary hiring and more flexible working hours for small and medium-sized firms. As a result of these reforms, the proportion of workers with fixed-term or training contracts increased substantially, from 6 percent of all employees in 1995 to 12 percent by 1997 (see Box 4 for a more detailed evaluation of labor market reforms in Argentina).

But further progress in deregulating the labor market was limited, and some new measures even reversed earlier reforms. In 1996, the government drafted legislation to further increase labor market flexibility and reduce labor costs—decentralizing the collective bargaining process by allowing wage negotiations at the firm rather than at the industry level; removing the *ultractividad* (a practice whereby collective agreements remain in effect until superseded by new arrangements); and replacing the costly system of severance payments by unemployment insurance based on individual accounts. In the event, the legislation met con-

---

[18]Throughout the second half of the 1990s close to 60 percent of banking-system assets and liabilities were denominated in dollars.

Box 4. Labor Market Reforms: How Much Was Done?

This box evaluates the Argentine labor market across a number of dimensions, including its fluidity, the opportunity cost of job search, the extent of job security regulations, the wage bargaining system, and the level of payroll taxes. It draws on cross-country evidence of the effects of labor market institutions and reforms.

Labor market fluidity

Reemployment rates for those employed on short-term contracts rose dramatically as a result of the 1995 reform, suggesting a fairly fluid labor market. Hopenhayn (2003) has estimated that reemployment rates rose by 40 percent, contributing to a relatively low incidence of long-term unemployment for Argentina during the 1990s (16 percent of unemployed in Argentina versus 45 percent for OECD countries with average unemployment over 10 percent). However, these figures are partly misleading because workers in Argentina move between employment and unemployment at regular intervals. Galiani and Hopenhayn (2003) have found that over a two-year period, 34 percent of Argentine unemployed spend more than one year in unemployment. Therefore, once the re-incidence of unemployment spells is taken into account, the incidence of long-term unemployment in Argentina is comparable to the incidence found in European economies.

The opportunity cost of job search

Argentina's policy of reducing severance pay for small firms in the 1995 reform was a step forward, although it would have been preferable to reduce severance pay across the board rather than to create a separate class of workers on fixed-term contracts. While the introduction of a limited number of fixed-term contracts is likely to increase flows through the labor market (which occurred in Argentina), the impact on unemployment is likely to be minimal because workers tend to switch from one temporary job to another. Blanchard and Landier (2001) found, in a different country context, that this type of reform results in more low productivity entry-level jobs, fewer regular jobs, and lower overall productivity and output.

Job security

Heckman and Pagés (2000) have calculated that Argentina ranks fairly high in terms of job security regulations. This assessment is based on a cost index, defined as the expected future cost of dismissing a worker. For Argentina, the cost is estimated at 25 percent of the annual wage, compared with zero in the United States and 15 percent in Brazil. Among a group of 36 Latin American, Caribbean, and OECD countries, only 12 have higher dismissal costs, including Mexico (26 percent) and Chile (28 percent). Although these figures do not take into account the increase in temporary and fixed-term contracts due to reforms in Argentina in the mid-90s, they still capture the marginal cost of dismissing a tenured worker.

The empirical literature on the effects of employment protection on the labor market and growth is mixed. Despite the existence of employment protection, unprofitable jobs are closed down and profitable ones start up at a reasonable rate in most countries. Some have argued that job security enhances productivity performance because productivity growth is often higher when employees are given some degree of autonomy in decision making (see Levine and Tyson, 1990). On the other hand, Di Tella and MacCulloch (1998) have shown using survey data that labor market flexibility increases employment. Although Argentina is not in their sample, it is possible to get an indirect estimate of the potential effects of less employment protection if we assume that Heckman's job protection index correlates with their index. Using the calculations of Di Tella and MacCulloch, it is estimated that the potential improvement in the Argentine labor market from increased flexibility could amount to an increase in employment of over 5 percent.

The wage bargaining system

Argentina's collective bargaining system is characterized by extensive protection and promotion of union activity. In the Argentine model, few unions are granted *personeria gremial* by the state, a special union status that confers a monopoly in representing workers in collective bargaining and strike. As a result, firm-based unions do not have union status if a higher-level union is organized and this scenario results in collective bargaining taking place at the industry level, generally found to be the least conducive to real wage adjustment (Calmfors and Driffill, 1988; and Thomas, 2002). Nickel and Denny (1990) have shown that the ability of unions to capture quasi rents has negative effects on investment and hence labor productivity. Moreover, Card and Freeman (2002) document that the elimination of Britain's productivity gap with France and Germany over the 1979–99 period is closely associated with the labor market reforms undertaken in the United Kingdom during the 1980s. In particular, they argue that the elimination of the productivity differential of about 10 percent between union and non-union workers could have contributed a 4.3 percent productivity gain over this period, corresponding to an annual improvement of 0.2 percentage points. Thomas has estimated average output growth differences between countries with flexible and rigid wages over the 1970–98 period and found that the difference was statistically significant at 0.3 percentage points of growth a year.

Payroll taxes

On the association between payroll tax changes and durable employment effects, the empirical evidence for Latin American countries is mixed. Gruber (1995)

Box 4 (concluded)

estimates that the reduced costs of payroll taxation to firms in Chile were fully passed on to workers in the form of higher wages following the pension reform in the early 1980s. In contrast, Edwards and Edwards (2000) argue that the reform might have contributed to lowering the unemployment rate between 2 and 3 percentage points. There are no unique studies for Argentina, but an analysis of the effect of job security and social security contributions on the employment-population ratio among Latin American countries revealed that a 1 percentage point decline in the payroll tax rate would lead to a 0.16 percentage point increase in the employment-population ratio. In Argentina's case, this would correspond to a 2 percentage point reduction in the unemployment rate following a 5 percent decline in the payroll tax rate, assuming the labor force remained constant. This result is comparable to findings on the Netherlands in the late 1980s and early 1990s by IMF staff, which indicated that the sensitivity of the wage to a 1 percentage point change in payroll taxation was 0.7 and that the sensitivity of employment to a 1 percent change in the real wage was 0.38. Combining these estimates at the average employment-population ratio for the Netherlands during the early 1990s would yield a 0.15 percentage point change for each 1 percent change in the payroll tax rate.

While the empirical analysis of the effects of labor market reform is not particularly robust, it is reasonable to argue that Argentina would have improved its labor market performance considerably if it had made it more flexible and reduced its associated tax burden. In particular, combining an increase in labor market flexibility to U.S. levels with a 5 percentage point reduction in the payroll tax rate could have halved the unemployment rate.

siderable resistance from unions and in Congress and was abandoned. The new law, passed in September 1998, represented a much-diluted version of the 1996 draft: although it did reduce dismissal costs, it retained the *ultractividad,* and actually promoted a further centralization of collective bargaining.[19] Moreover, while the payroll tax was reduced from 49 percent of gross earnings in the early 1990s to 43 percent by 2000, it remained high by international standards.

As a result, despite the reforms of the 1990s that boosted labor productivity in the industrial sector and improved cost competitiveness, Argentina's labor market was not flexible enough to prevent a large rise in the unemployment rate. Labor productivity growth averaged a solid 3 percent a year during 1991–98, with especially strong gains in the industrial sector (Figure 7). The latter was driven by a declining industrial workforce, particularly in the earlier stages of liberalization.[20] At the same time, industrial sector wage growth remained restrained, even though Argentina's collective bargaining system encouraged industry-level agreements—a practice generally found to be the least conducive to real wage moderation[21]—the nominal wage per worker in the industrial sector declined by 1 percent a year between 1994 and 1998, with unit labor costs falling by about 20 percent over this period.[22] However, labor market flexibility continued to be hampered by various legislative barriers, resulting in insufficient job creation. Indeed, although the drop in industrial sector employment in the first half of the 1990s was largely offset by new jobs created in the services sector, this was not sufficient to absorb a rapidly rising labor force. As a consequence, the unemployment rate doubled to 12 percent by 1994 and did not subsequently fall below this level (Figure 8). Moreover, economy-wide productivity growth trickled to zero in the second half of the decade, accompanied by a surge in public sector employment, while employment creation in the private sector was disappointing. In short, while some wage adjustment clearly did take place, it was insufficient to absorb a growing pool of unemployed.

Currency Board

The currency board was widely viewed as providing needed monetary stability after a long history of monetized fiscal deficits, high inflation, and low and volatile growth. But it was an inherently risky regime: it sacrificed the ability to use the exchange rate as an adjustment tool and constrained the authorities' ability to alter monetary policy, with the potential of creating in-

---

[19]In 2000, the new government reversed some elements of this law, authorizing dominance of collective agreements at the enterprise level over those at the sectoral level, and extending the trial period for subsidized labor contracts from one month to three months.

[20]During 1990–94, employment in the manufacturing sector fell by about 20 percent.

[21]Heckman and Pagés (2000); Calmfors and Driffill (1998); and Thomas (2002).

[22]Caution is required in making strong inferences about the magnitude of wage adjustment, however, as there are questions about the quality of wage data in Argentina. Galiani's (2001) analysis of micro data from the labor force survey suggests that the average nominal wage in the Buenos Aires area declined by 14 percent between 1994 and 2000, which compares with a 4 percent decline on the basis of official numbers from the National Institute of Statistics.

Figure 7. Productivity and Wages

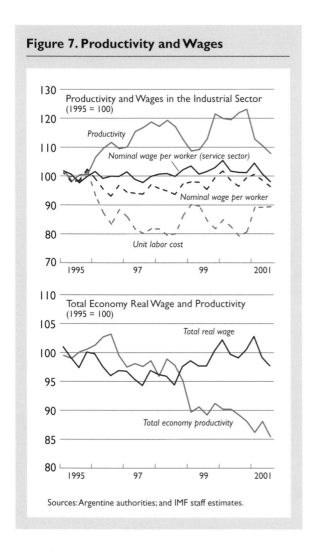

Sources: Argentine authorities; and IMF staff estimates.

Figure 8. Labor Market Characteristics

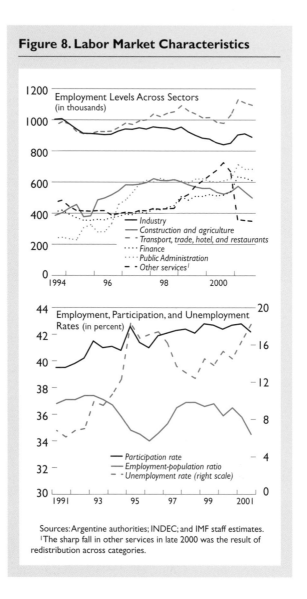

Sources: Argentine authorities; INDEC; and IMF staff estimates.
[1] The sharp fall in other services in late 2000 was the result of redistribution across categories.

consistencies between monetary and fiscal policies and/or procyclical monetary conditions.

Under a currency board arrangement, a government is precluded from money financing of the deficit and would face a static constraint on its budget deficit if it were unable to issue debt. But this was not the case in Argentina, where the government was able to borrow amply both domestically and internationally. Thus, the currency board imposed a direct constraint only on fiscal policy, once creditors became concerned about the government's solvency and unwilling to provide new financing. These considerations find reflection in recent theories of the "fiscal determination" of the price level, which suggest that a fixed exchange rate regime—*a fortiori,* a currency board arrangement—is viable only if the *dynamics* of fiscal policy are sufficiently flexible (Box 5). In the parlance of this literature, a fixed exchange rate requires a "money dominant" regime—that is, fiscal policy must adjust so that the govern-

ment's present value budget constraint is expected to be satisfied at a price level consistent with the fixed exchange rate. While this does not rule out the use of fiscal policy as a stabilization tool under a fixed exchange rate regime, it does imply the need for a prudent fiscal policy in good times since any fiscal expansion during a downturn is constrained by the requirement that the public sector's solvency be satisfied at the given price level.

The currency board arrangement remained viable as long as there was sufficient political will to subordinate fiscal policy to maintaining the peg—in the sense of having a "money dominant" regime. While arguably this was the case during the early years of stabilization, the rising level of public indebtedness suggests that, at least at some point during the decade, Argentina slipped into a "fiscal

---

Box 5. Fiscal Discipline and the Viability of the Exchange Rate Regime

As noted in the text, under a fixed exchange rate regime, a government that cannot issue debt faces a static constraint on its budget deficit because the exchange rate peg limits monetary financing of the deficit. But Argentina's public sector could issue debt both domestically and in international capital markets. Of greater relevance, therefore, are the implications of theories of the "fiscal determination" of the price level, as applied to the exchange rate regime.[1] This theory emphasizes that a fixed exchange rate regime will be viable only to the extent that the dynamics of the public finances are sufficiently flexible.

The focal point of this literature is the intertemporal budget constraint of the consolidated public sector (including the central bank). A "no-Ponzi game" constraint, which requires that the present value of outstanding obligations be non-positive, implies that:

$$\frac{D_t + M_t}{P_t} = E_t\left\{\sum_{j=0}^{\infty} \frac{(s_{t+j} + \theta_{t+j})}{(1+r)^j}\right\} \qquad (1)$$

where D_t is the nominal stock of outstanding government debt inherited at the beginning of period t, M_t is the nominal stock of money (net of the central bank's foreign exchange reserves and credit to the economy) inherited at the beginning of period t, P is the price level, s is the primary surplus and θ is central bank seigniorage

[1] On the fiscal determination of the price level, see Woodford (1994) and (1995); on the application of this theory to the exchange rate regime, see Canzoneri, Cumby, and Diba (1998) who provide a more general formulation of (1) under the assumption that the economy's discount rate is not constant.

(in real terms), $(1 + r)$ is the economy's discount factor, and $E\{\bullet\}$ is the expectations operator.

Assuming that the public sector does not repudiate its obligations (either bonds or base money), the intertemporal budget constraint (1) must be satisfied. But there are two ways in which this may happen. In a **money-dominant** regime, the price level is determined, and it is the stream of primary surpluses on the right-hand-side of the equation that must adjust to maintain the government's solvency. In a **fiscal-dominant** regime, the stream of future primary surpluses is given, and it is the price level that must adjust to ensure that the government's present value budget constraint is satisfied.

Under a pegged exchange rate, the domestic price level is determined by the exchange rate (for instance, by purchasing power parity or—more generally—by the requirement that the exchange rate not become uncompetitive) and cannot, in general, adjust to satisfy (1). Therefore, to be viable, an exchange rate peg requires that macroeconomic policies operate under a "money dominant" regime.

The theory has a number of implications that are of direct relevance to Argentina's experience. In particular, the larger the initial stock of debt, D, the more difficult it is to satisfy the present value budget constraint without an increase in the price level—that is, without a devaluation of the exchange rate. Moreover, to the extent that the price level is required to fall (to restore competitiveness following an increase in the nominal effective exchange rate), the left-hand side of the equation increases, requiring correspondingly larger primary surpluses to satisfy the intertemporal budget constraint.

---

dominant" regime, ultimately dooming the currency board arrangement.

More generally, while the currency board undoubtedly played an essential part in the successful disinflation of the early 1990s, it is questionable whether the regime was an appropriate longer-term arrangement for Argentina. Given the structure of the Argentine economy, including its size, lack of openness, export concentration, and labor market rigidities, the case for maintaining the pegged exchange rate regime beyond the macroeconomic stabilization phase is not compelling. Indeed, a probit analysis of the choice between pegged or floating regimes, based on countries' structural characteristics, generates an implied probability for a peg in Argentina of only 40–50 percent, compared with an average of about 70 percent for other countries that maintained a peg.[23] Moreover, the implied probability is signifi-

[23] The results are based on a model developed in Ghosh, Gulde, and Wolf (2002).

cantly higher (around 90 percent) for most smaller currency board countries, such as Estonia or members of the East Caribbean Central Bank (ECCB), though not for some of the larger, more export-diversified countries with currency boards.

Yet abandoning the currency board would have been far from costless. Part of the currency board's credibility stemmed from the high cost—both economic and political—of exiting the regime. The most commonly cited costs of exiting a currency board (compared with a simple exchange rate peg) are the legal and institutional changes required. But of greater importance were the implications of the widespread dollarization of assets and liabilities. Dollarization may to some extent have been encouraged by the currency board itself, although the evidence is not conclusive (Box 6). Moreover, dollarization was to some extent encouraged by the financial regulatory framework associated with the currency board: consistent with the premise that the dollar-

Box 6. Did the Currency Board Contribute to Dollarization?

A commonly asserted proposition is that Argentina's currency board arrangement contributed to dollarization of the economy, in the sense that a large proportion of the banking system's assets and liabilities were denominated in dollars (see the Figure). The argument harkens back to the East Asian crisis, where *de jure* or *de facto* exchange rate pegs were said to have encouraged dollar-denominated borrowing by reducing nominal exchange rate uncertainty. But neither the theoretical arguments nor the empirical evidence in favor of this proposition is especially compelling.

Dollarization is usually a reaction to monetary instability and a lack of confidence in the domestic currency, which induces individuals to want to hold U.S. dollars or dollar deposits as a store of value. Yet, if an exchange rate peg is credible, it should increase confidence in the domestic currency and thus decrease dollarization. In Argentina, for instance, the currency board arrangement made the peso (almost) "as good as the dollar." Of course, short of replacing the domestic currency entirely, there will always be some risk premium on the domestic currency. In Argentina, over the period 1993–1998, the spread between peso- and U.S. dollar-denominated loans averaged less than 2 percentage points per year (though it was considerably larger in the immediate aftermath of the Tequila crisis).

One argument is that, to the extent that borrowers believe the peg will be maintained, they have the incentive to borrow in dollars, thus avoiding the risk premium on domestic-currency-denominated loans. In this sense, the fixed exchange rate regime could indeed encourage dollarization. The problem with this argument is that it is not logically consistent: if the peg is indeed credible, households will not want to hold dollar-denominated deposits, on which they receive a lower interest rate. Thus, the argument can normally not account for both extensive dollar-denominated borrowing and widespread holdings of dollar deposits. However, when doubts about the peg encourage holding of dollar deposits, households and firms may still have an incentive to borrow in dollars, if they expect to be bailed out (or simply default) in the event of a large devaluation. (Alternatively, borrowers may have anticipated government intervention to limit their exposure in the event of a devaluation—as indeed happened through the asymmetric pesoization.)

The empirical evidence is equally equivocal. A regression of the share of foreign currency deposits on the exchange rate regime (using a panel dataset of 88 mainly emerging market countries during the 1990s, 606 observations in total) actually yields a negative and statistically significant coefficient estimate for pegged exchange rate regimes. A pegged exchange rate regime is associated with a 12 percentage point lower share of foreign-currency deposits relative to floating regimes (and a 2 percentage point lower share relative to intermediate regimes).[1] In contrast to the cross-country

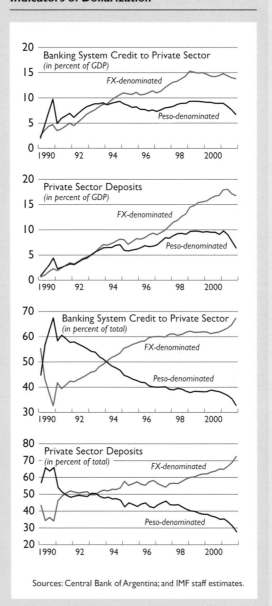

Indicators of Dollarization

Sources: Central Bank of Argentina; and IMF staff estimates.

experience, in Argentina, the share of foreign-currency deposits to total deposits increased during the 1990s, suggesting that country-specific factors were at play, including, perhaps, the expectation that the government would intervene if the currency board collapsed.

---

[1] Not controlling for country-specific effects, the coefficient on pegged regimes is −10.98 (t-statistic: 5.05***), while the coefficient on inflation is 0.44 (t-statistic: 2.76*); controlling for country-fixed effects, the coefficient on the pegged regime dummy becomes −11.98 (t-statistic: 2.07**), where one, two, and three asterisks denote statistical significance at the 10, 5, and 1 percent levels, respectively.

peso link was permanent and irrevocable, the regulators did not impose restrictions on currency mismatches.[24] By the late 1990s, with more than one-half of banks' assets and liabilities and 90 percent of the public debt denominated in foreign currency (mainly U.S. dollars), abandoning the currency board arrangement would have been extremely disruptive to the economy—as indeed it turned out to be. The loss of policy credibility also tended to discourage an early exit. Indeed, given the various crises afflicting emerging market countries, including the Mexican devaluation in 1994, the Asian crises in 1997–98, the Russian default in 1998, and the Brazilian devaluation in 1998–99, there were relatively few opportunities to exit the regime at a time when there was no turbulence in international capital markets.

Based on these considerations, it would likely have been desirable to exit the currency board during a non-crisis period, when the exit could have been accomplished in a more orderly way. This would have meant exiting sometime between 1992 and the first half of 1994, or between 1996 and early 1997. But any talk of a possible exit met with fierce resistance: the economy was performing well during those periods, and there was strong support, both by the authorities and the public, for maintaining the currency board. As a result, the country found itself in a quandary, unable to muster the political support to tackle the public debt dynamics and commit unequivocally to a "money dominant" regime, yet unwilling to make a decisive break from the currency board arrangement, which was providing much needed policy credibility and allowing Argentina to continue to tap international capital markets despite its growing indebtedness.

Summary

Despite the boom, the Argentine economy became increasingly vulnerable to crisis during the 1990s. The chief locus of vulnerability was the increase in public sector indebtedness; the main structural deficiencies were the low share and high concentration of exports, the economy's reliance on external savings, and the lack of labor market flexibility. At the same time, heavy reliance on foreign-currency-denominated borrowing and generally high dollarization raised the stakes associated with an eventual exit from the currency board. These weaknesses, which were not sufficiently addressed in IMF-supported programs during this time, had an importance beyond their individual implications: in combination, and particularly in the context of the currency board regime, they represented growing vulnerability to a sudden downturn—which eventually transpired in the latter half of 1998.

---

[24]The absence of such restrictions also, in the short run, eased pressures on the currency board itself, by loosening the link between peso deposits and base money.

III   Downturn and Deepening Depression: 1998–2000

Following a robust recovery from the 1995 Tequila crisis, and strong growth in 1997, the economy slid into depression in the latter half of 1998. This depression lasted throughout the entire pre-crisis period and deepened, as the policy dilemma became increasingly apparent to the markets and binding to the government.

Initial Downturn—1998

The downturn was triggered by a variety of factors, including a cyclical correction, political uncertainty, and contagion from Russia and then Brazil (Box 7). These factors resulted in a severe contraction of private consumption and investment spending (Figure 9). Output growth, which had reached 8 percent in 1997, declined to less than 4 percent in 1998, falling at an annual rate of more than 10 percent during the fourth quarter. The downturn was to some degree a correction, given that the economy had been running above potential for some time, with GDP an estimated 3 percentage points above its full employment level in early 1998. A related cyclical factor was the unwinding of adjustments in the stock of durables.

The proximate trigger for the downturn was financial contagion from the Russian crisis in August 1998. Beginning in the fourth quarter of 1998, private debt-creating capital inflows, which had averaged more than 2 percent of GDP in 1996–97, turned negative (Figure 10).[25] At the same time, spreads on Argentine sovereign bonds rose from about 500 basis points in July to 750 basis points in December. This had repercussions for domestic interest rates. Between the first half of 1998 and early 1999, prime lending rates on both U.S. dollar- and peso-denominated loans rose by 2 to 3 percentage points (to 10 percent and 12 percent, respectively), implying an increase in real interest rates by some 5 percentage points to 13 percent (11 percent on dollar loans). The

currency board arrangement, however, muted the impact of the external shock on the domestic economy. Argentina's spreads rose by less than half of the average increase in emerging market bond spreads (EMBI), and the increase in real domestic lending rates was significantly lower than in Mexico, for example, though comparable with that in Chile.[26]

Heightened political uncertainty also helped to puncture consumer confidence and dampen private sector spending. Historically, political crises in Argentina have had a significant impact on economic growth.[27] Although President Carlos Menem's ascendancy to power in 1989 brought some political stability, the situation became more uncertain in 1998 with his attempts to remain in power for an unprecedented third term, despite an explicit constitutional prohibition and public opinion polls indicating widespread opposition. The success of the Alianza party—an electoral coalition between the two main opposition parties—in the congressional elections of 1997 (winning 46 percent of the vote compared with the Peronists' 36 percent) was a threat to the ruling party. Indeed, the opposition's success was a key factor in Menem's decision to rule himself out of the race for the Peronist leadership in July 1998, when it became clear that his re-election proposal risked splitting the party. This contributed to a further weakening of the government's command of the country's political and economic affairs.

The adverse consequences of political uncertainty and financial contagion were compounded by a series of external shocks, including the decline in demand for Argentina's exports associated with Brazil's 1998–99 crisis; the effect on competitiveness of the depreciation of the real; and a 6 percent terms-of-trade deterioration—stemming, in part, from a sharp decline in world prices for Argentina's

---

[25]Total capital inflows remained positive, albeit declining, until 2001. This mainly reflects large foreign direct investment projects that were already in the pipeline.

[26]Lending rates in Mexico increased from 22 to 35 percent (12 percentage points in real terms) while Chile's rates rose from 17 percent to 24 percent (5 percentage points in real terms).

[27]Also, according to data collected by Burns on political crises across the world, Argentina averaged a major government crisis each year over the 1970–90 period compared to a worldwide average of one crisis every five years.

Box 7. Factors Contributing to the 1998 Downturn

Various factors gave rise to the sharp downturn in Argentina that began in mid-1998, including a cyclical correction following rapid growth in 1996 and 1997, a sharp downward adjustment in purchases of durables, an increase in political uncertainty, and dipping consumer confidence. Appendix I indicates that various measures of potential output yield an excess demand gap of more than 3 percent of GDP in 1998. Moreover, while automobile consumption rose rapidly in 1993 and 1994, and again in 1996 and 1997, in response to the stable inflationary environment, a sharp downward adjustment took place in 1999 and 2000, associated with the fact that purchasers of automobiles had by then upgraded their stock. The sharp decline in durables consumption had a noticeable effect on total private consumption.

One of the triggers for the growth slowdown was the increase in political uncertainty associated with President Menem's desire to remain in power for an unprecedented third term. In recent years, a number of researchers have considered the relationship between political instability and growth, arguing that political instability increases uncertainty and, thereby, has negative effects on productive economic decisions such as investment and saving, and ultimately on growth (Alesina and others, 1996; Alesina, and Perotti 1995). To quantify such an impact, the Ghosh and Phillips (1998) growth model was re-estimated with the addition of a variable incorporating the number of government crises in each country based on Burns' dataset. Argentina has had many political crises over the past 30 years, and including separate political crisis coefficients for Argentina and for the rest of the world yields significant differences. Indeed, the estimates reveal that a political crisis

would lower per capita growth by 2 percentage points in Argentina compared with only ¾ percentage point in the rest of the world. Of course, these calibrations make no allowance for the severity of different political crises, and to the extent that the 1998 crisis was comparatively mild, its isolated impact on GDP growth would be smaller.

Another trigger for the slowdown was the effect of the Russian default on emerging market bond prices, which affected not only private investment in Argentina, through higher financing costs, but also consumption, in the context of a close relationship between consumer confidence and the sovereign debt spread (see figure).

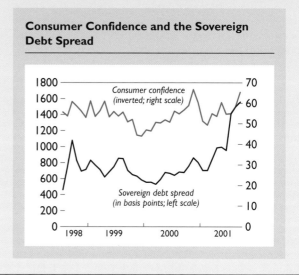

Consumer Confidence and the Sovereign Debt Spread

commodity exports. As a result, Argentina's export earnings fell by 10 percent in the second half of 1998 (relative to the first half), while growth in volume terms was reduced to less than 2 percent from 15 percent in 1997.

While the direct impact on output growth of the slowdown of exports was limited by the low share of exports in the economy, the combination of shocks heightened concerns about the resilience of the Argentine economy in general. With exports comprising only one-tenth of the economy, their weakening had little direct effect on real GDP growth. Nevertheless, to the extent that the external shocks contributed to rising real interest rates and a weakening in confidence, they played an important role in the sharp contraction in domestic demand. More specifically, the external shocks and subsequent real effective appreciation of the peso following the devaluation of the real in early 1999 (over 14 percent in real terms, on the basis of both consumer price inflation

and unit labor cost) threw into sharper relief the precariousness of the public sector and external indebtedness, and the trap the economy had fallen into. As long as the nominal exchange rate remained strong in effective terms (reflecting both the peg to an appreciating U.S. dollar and the depreciation of the Brazilian real), restoring competitiveness would require price deflation. This, of course, would weaken economic activity to the extent that nominal wages and prices in the economy were downward inflexible (Box 8). Moreover, as elaborated in the following section, a real depreciation, whether through an exchange rate adjustment or price deflation, would have likely worsened the debt ratios. Such concerns were one factor behind the persistence of the increase in spreads on Argentine bonds, even as spreads in other emerging market countries in the region began narrow in mid-1999. In turn, these wider spreads and higher interest rates contributed to the continuing economic malaise.

Figure 9. Contributions to Output Growth
(Seasonally adjusted, in percent per quarter)

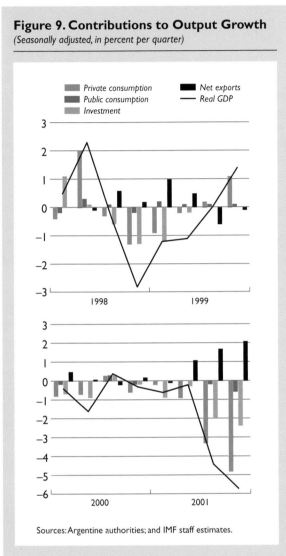

Sources: Argentine authorities; and IMF staff estimates.

Figure 10. Capital Market Indicators

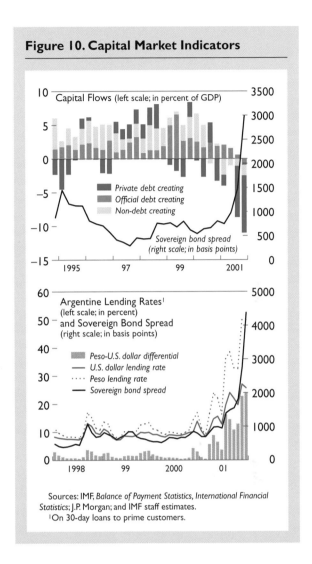

Sources: IMF, *Balance of Payment Statistics, International Financial Statistics*; J.P. Morgan; and IMF staff estimates.
[1] On 30-day loans to prime customers.

Deepening Depression and Policy Dilemma: 1999–2000

Once the economy entered depression, it seemed unable to escape. Output shrank by 3½ percent in 1999 and by a further 1 percent in 2000, with deflationary pressures leading consumer prices to fall by some 1 to 2 percent both in 1999 and in 2000. Reflecting labor market rigidities, real wages rose by 2½ percent in 1999 despite the economic downturn and by a further 2 percent in 2000. Unemployment increased from 12½ percent in the second half of 1998 (its lowest level since the Tequila crisis) to 14½ percent in the first half of 1999, and 15 percent by 2000. At the same time, the public sector deficit rose to more than 4 percent of GDP in 1999, and 3½ percent in 2000, while the public debt ratio increased by

10 percentage points to more than 50 percent of GDP. However, in contrast to earlier years, when off-budget expenditures had played a major role, the debt dynamics were now driven mainly by an adverse differential between interest rates and growth.

The government's initial attempts at curbing its growing deficit were at best timid, and the fiscal policy stance became clearly contractionary only in 2000. Public expenditure grew by some 4¼ percent in real terms in 1999 and by more than 5 percent at the provincial level. Helped by a rise in the revenue ratio, the fiscal impulse was mildly contractionary, but due to the operation of automatic stabilizers the primary balance deteriorated by 1¼ percentage points to a deficit of ¾ percent of GDP. Along with rising interest payments, the overall deficit doubled to more than 4 percent of GDP—a slippage of 2½ percentage points relative to the program target (Table 4). In light of the fiscal deterioration in 1999,

Box 8. Deflation and Depression

Pinpointing the precise mechanisms through which the currency board may have contributed to the recession is difficult. The behavior of real interest rates or monetary aggregates, for instance, seems to provide only a peripheral explanation. Nevertheless, the fixed exchange rate regime implied that corrections to the real exchange rate could take place only through price deflation. One hypothesis, therefore, is that since a little inflation may help "grease the wheels" of the economy, deflation itself contributed to weakness in economic activity. Consistent with this, Ghosh and Phillips (1998) find that, while high inflation is associated with poor growth performance, at very low inflation rates, increases in the rate are associated with higher output growth. They estimate a "kink" at around $2\frac{1}{2}$ percent per year (model 1). An alternative formulation (model 2) puts the kink at negative inflation rates. Using an annual cross-country panel dataset, these two models are estimated.

The standard growth determinants are generally of the expected signs. Intermediate exchange rate regimes are associated with higher growth, as is a higher investment ratio, greater trade openness, positive terms of trade shocks, a higher human capital stock (as measured by the average number of years of schooling), a lower average tax ratio, lower initial income (due to "convergence"), lower population growth, and larger economic size (as proxied by population). Higher inflation is associated with lower growth, but deflation is also associated with lower growth (model 2), with the deleterious effect stronger the higher the deflation rate.

Since Argentina experienced deflation of (at most) 2 percent per year, these estimates suggest that due to the deflation, real GDP growth was between $\frac{1}{2}$ and $1\frac{1}{2}$ percent per year lower than it otherwise would have been. However, some caution is required in applying these estimates. Since the regression commingles all the effects that tight monetary policy might have, including for instance through high real interest rates, this effect should not be added to other effects.

	Model 1		Model 2	
	Coefficient	t-stat.	Coefficient	t-stat.
Constant	0.006	1.38	0.006	1.36
Pegged	0.002	0.60	0.002	0.56
Intermediate	0.007	2.66***	0.007	2.68***
Investment ratio	0.033	1.50	0.034	1.53
Openness ratio	0.010	3.38***	0.010	3.39***
Terms of trade	0.031	2.36**	0.031	2.34**
Years of schooling	0.002	3.55***	0.002	3.47***
Tax ratio	−0.018	−1.77*	−0.020	−1.89*
Budget balance	0.003	0.12	0.003	0.13
Initial income	−0.028	−5.06***	−0.028	−5.10***
Population growth	−0.579	−5.29***	−0.582	−5.33***
Population size	0.004	4.85***	0.004	4.85***
Inflation	−0.053	−4.99***	−0.053	−5.02***
Inflation (below 2.5 percent per year)	**0.165**	1.53		
Inflation (below 0 percent per year)			**0.706**	2.55**
Number of observations,	1763		1763	
R^2	0.19		0.19	

Note: Asterisks indicate statistical significance at the 1(***), 5(**), and 10(*) percent levels.

the 2000 IMF-supported program sought to reduce the overall public sector deficit to $2\frac{1}{4}$ percent of GDP (and $1\frac{1}{2}$ percent of GDP in 2001). However, despite a sizable structural tightening of 2 percentage points of GDP, in line with the program target, the deficit fell by merely $\frac{1}{2}$ percentage point of GDP, and the government's gross financing needs rose to US$26 billion, or more than 9 percent of GDP.[28]

Against this background, the government faced a harsh policy dilemma, as the buildup of debt in the earlier years had eliminated any room for stimulating the economy through fiscal expansion. From a cyclical perspective, fiscal and monetary expansion

---

[28]The calibrated fiscal impulse (i.e., the structural fiscal adjustment), while sensitive to uncertain potential output growth assumptions, provides a more appropriate assessment of policies than developments in the actual balance, which were dominated by the economic downturn. The impulse estimates in Table 4 are based on potential output growth of about $2\frac{1}{2}$ percent (see Appendix I) and would be some $\frac{1}{4}$ percentage point higher (i.e., a smaller withdrawal) or lower, respectively, for every 1 percentage point reduction or increase in assumed potential output growth.

Table 4. Programmed and Actual Fiscal Balances and Impulses, 1999–2001
(In percent of GDP, unless otherwise indicated)

	Fiscal Balance			Primary Fiscal Balance			Public Debt	Real GDP Growth (in percent)	Impulse	Implied Impulse[1]
	Federal	Provincial	Total	Federal	Provincial	Total				
1999										
Second review (Feb. 1999)[2]	−1.0	−0.5	−1.5	1.5	−0.1	1.4	43.0	2.5	−0.8	−2.6
Third review EFF (May 1999)[2]	−1.8	−0.6	−2.4	1.1	−0.2	0.9	46.1	−1.5	−1.3	−1.8
Actual	−2.5	−1.6	−4.1	0.4	−1.1	−0.7	47.6	−3.4	−0.2	−0.2
2000										
Original program (Feb. 2000)	−1.6	−0.7	−2.3	1.6	−0.2	1.3	47.7	3.4	−1.8	−3.2
First review (Sept. 2000)	−1.9	−1.0	−2.9	1.4	−0.4	1.0	49.4	0.9	−2.0	−2.6
Actual	−2.5	−1.2	−3.6	0.9	−0.5	0.4	50.9	−0.8	−1.9	−1.9
2001										
Original program (Feb. 2000)	−0.9	−0.5	−1.4	...	...	2.7	47.3	3.7	−1.1[3]	−3.4
First review (Sept. 2000)	−1.4	−0.6	−2.0	...	...	2.4	49.6	3.7	−1.1[3]	−3.4
Second review (Jan. 2001)	−2.2	−0.9	−3.1	1.7	−0.1	1.5	52.5	2.5	−1.1	−3.0
Third review (May 2001)	−2.2	−0.9	−3.2	1.7	−0.1	1.6	53.4	2.0	−1.3	−3.0
Fourth review (August 2001)	−2.4	−1.0	−3.3	1.6	0.0	1.5	56.9	−1.4	−2.0	−2.8
Actual	−4.4	−1.9	−6.3	0.1	−1.5	−1.4	62.2	−4.5	0.1	0.1

[1] Impulse that would have resulted if the program balance had been achieved (through expenditure adjustments) with the actual growth outcome.

[2] Figures in percent of GDP deviate from those in IMF staff reports due to subsequent revisions in GDP data.

[3] As a breakdown between revenue and expenditure is not available, the impulse is estimated by assuming that the revenue ratio in 2001 is the same as the projected ratio for 2000.

would clearly have been appropriate, but the former would have been associated with a larger fiscal financing requirement that would have driven up interest rates even further, while the latter was limited by the currency board arrangement.[29] Indeed, even without such a rise in interest rates, and the optimistic assumption of a large fiscal multiplier effect on output, a wider deficit would almost surely have increased not just the overall level of public debt but also its ratio to GDP (Box 9). In the event, IMF-supported programs in 1999–2001 targeted primary surpluses in the range of 1 to 2¾ percent of GDP, though actual outcomes fell far short of these targets. The result was perhaps the worst of both worlds: fiscal policy failed to provide a decisive positive impulse to the economy, and confidence was probably undermined by the continual slippages of fiscal targets, resulting in rising public sector indebtedness and higher interest rate premiums.

A key aspect underlying the fiscal underperformance was the disappointing outturn of both real GDP growth and inflation relative to projections. Both program projections and consensus forecasts in 1999–2001 repeatedly assumed that growth would recover and that there would be some positive inflation (Figure 11). Had it been known that growth and

---

[29]In fact, the design of the Argentine exchange rate regime allowed for greater leeway in altering monetary policy than would have been possible under a "pure" currency board arrangement (where changes in base money can occur only through movements of the central bank's foreign exchange reserves). In Argentina, the central bank (BCRA) could engage in currency and bond swap operations as well as repos and reverse repos with banks. In addition, a discounting facility, whereby the BCRA rediscounted securities and commercial paper from banks at interest rates above the repo rate, served as a limited lender-of-last-resort function. Reflecting the leeway under Argentina's currency board arrangement, the correlation (over the period 1993:Q1–2001:Q4) between net foreign assets of the central bank and reserve money was only 0.08 and the correlation between the changes in these variables was only 0.45 (instead of unity).

Box 9. Could Expansionary Fiscal Policy Have Stabilized the Debt Dynamics?

Some commentators have claimed that fiscal tightening, by further weakening activity, exacerbated Argentina's debt dynamics, hastening the onset of the crisis.[1] To assess this claim, it is useful to consider under what circumstances a widening of the deficit could reduce the debt ratio. Starting from the standard expression for debt dynamics:

$$\dot{d} = (r - g)\,d + p$$

where d is the debt-to-GDP ratio, r is the real interest rate, g is the real growth rate of the economy, and p is the primary deficit, a larger primary deficit reduces the debt-to-GDP ratio if:

$$\partial(\dot{d})/\partial p < 0 \Rightarrow (r_p - g_p)\,d + 1 < 0.$$

A key parameter is the response of interest rates to the wider deficit. Assuming that there is no response, the above condition reduces to: $g_p > (1 \, / \, d)$. That is, the response of output growth to a larger primary deficit must be greater than the reciprocal of the debt ratio; at end-1999, the latter was $1/0.47 = 2.12$.

The most generous framework to the case for a fiscal expansion is a Keynesian model in which output is fully demand-determined. While such a framework does not lend itself easily to addressing output growth, by evaluating the policy around an initial growth rate of zero (a reasonable assumption for this exercise), it is possible to interpret the increase in output from the boost to aggregate demand as the change in the growth rate.

Under a Keynesian model, the output response to an increase in government spending is given by

$$\frac{\Delta y}{y} = \frac{1}{1 - c + m}\,\frac{\Delta g}{y}$$

where c is the marginal propensity to consume and m is the marginal propensity to import.[2] Point estimates for the marginal propensities to consume and import (estimated over the period 1991–2001) are

0.657 and 0.187, respectively, yielding

$$\frac{1}{1 - c + m} = \frac{1}{1 - 0.657 + 0.187} = 1.88$$

—shy of the critical value of 2.12.

In other words, even in the most favorable circumstances, a fiscal expansion would not have helped stabilize the debt ratio. Moreover, to the extent that the recession was not purely an aggregate demand shock, but also reflected slower growth of potential output, the response to the fiscal expansion would have been smaller.

The above calculation is also predicated on the larger fiscal deficit not triggering a rise in interest rates. Although effective interest rates on government debt rose

steadily from 6.3 percent per year in 1997 when the public sector deficit was 2 percent of GDP to 9.0 percent per year by 2001 when the public sector deficit reached almost 7 percent of GDP, it is difficult to distinguish the impact on interest rates of the widening deficit from the effects on confidence of the general deterioration of macroeconomic conditions. In particular, it is at least theoretically possible that the announcement of a wider deficit—by presaging a stimulus to economic activity—would boost confidence so much that interest rates would fall. Conversely, the wider deficit might erode confidence further, implying higher interest rates. While the evidence is equivocal, an "event study" analysis suggests that Argentina's spreads relative to benchmark U.S. bonds increased in response to news of wider fiscal deficits (see figure), although the pattern of Argentina's spreads relative to the emerging market bond index (EMBI) is more supportive of the opposite conclusion (arguably, however, the latter spread is of less relevance for the evolution of Argentina's debt dynamics).

As is readily verified, to the extent that the wider deficit elicits higher interest rates, $r_p > 0$, the condition for an expansionary fiscal policy to stabilize the debt ratio becomes more difficult to satisfy.

Argentine Bonds Relative to U.S. Bonds, Three-week Moving Average

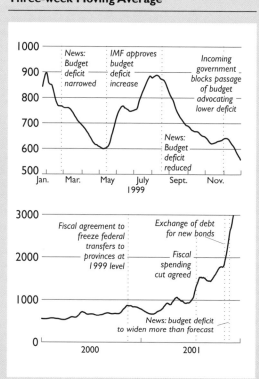

---

[1] See Stiglitz (2002).

[2] If there are income taxes, the multiplier is smaller: $\Delta y \, / \, \Delta g = (1 - c(1 - \tau) + m)^{-1}$.

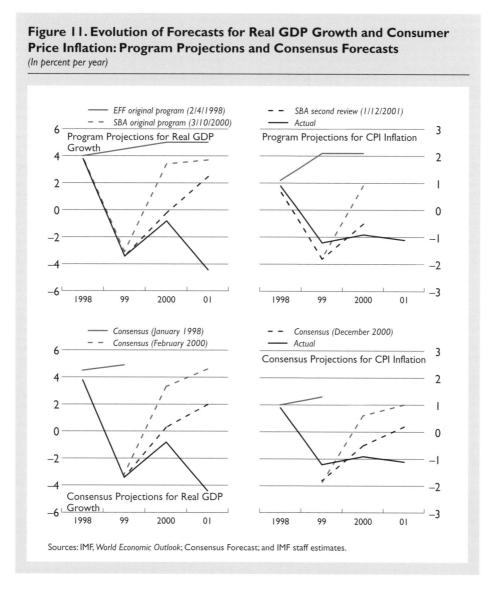

Figure 11. Evolution of Forecasts for Real GDP Growth and Consumer Price Inflation: Program Projections and Consensus Forecasts
(In percent per year)

Sources: IMF, *World Economic Outlook*; Consensus Forecast; and IMF staff estimates.

inflation were going to be lower, the need for fiscal adjustment might have been clearer since the projected debt ratio (given the lower nominal GDP) would have been correspondingly higher. Conversely, to the extent that a prolonged recession was projected, there would have been more calls for providing a fiscal stimulus to boost activity. Thus, whether more accurate projections would have resulted in a very different policy stance is debatable. That said, the continued fiscal underperformance probably undermined confidence in the authorities' ability to deliver on agreed targets.[30] The error in

projecting positive inflation may have been of even greater consequence given that, under the program, nominal wages were supposed to adjust downward to restore external competitiveness. Inasmuch as positive inflation was projected for 2000 and 2001 by both IMF staff and private forecasters, workers were likely to hold similar expectations, making them less willing to accept lower nominal wages.

Other than the fiscal stance, the key decision facing the authorities was whether to abandon the currency board and adopt an alternative monetary and exchange rate regime. Clearly, the authorities' ability to address the crisis would have been greater in the absence of a currency board—that is, if it had taken the opportunity to exit in non-crises times earlier in the decade. Moreover, given that the currency board was ultimately abandoned, it is not clear that there

---

[30]This may be contrasted to the experience in East Asia, where the sustainability of public finances was much less of a concern, and where fiscal targets were rapidly loosened as it became clear that activity was going to be much weaker than originally projected. See Lane and others (1999).

was any benefit from delaying the exit. But by the time the recession was under way, changing the currency regime would, *by itself,* have given little relief from the crushing debt dynamics; on the contrary, it would have immediately worsened the situation given the foreign-currency exposures of public and private balance sheets.

Abandoning the currency board in 1999 or 2000 would have provided little relief on financing costs, and would have been unlikely to rescue the economy from the slump. A convenient way of characterizing the monetary policy stance as constrained by the currency board is through the use of a monetary conditions index, which is a weighted average of real exchange rate and real interest rate movements relative to a base period when the economy is in internal equilibrium at full employment (Box 10). The first panel in the Box 10 figure presents this index for Argentina and shows that it has a close relationship with the output gap. Indeed, the fit is remarkably strong and swift so that sudden movements in the monetary policy stance are rapidly mirrored in output movements. The procyclical tightening of monetary conditions during the recession is illustrated by the substantial rise in the monetary conditions indices (MCI) beginning in 1998, with an even sharper rise during 2001. The second panel in the box figure qualifies this result, comparing MCI indices for Argentina, Chile, and Mexico; here, it is noteworthy that in Mexico, with a flexible exchange rate, monetary conditions also tightened from 1998 through the end of 2000, although they did not mirror Argentina's sharp tightening during 2001. This suggests that the tightening Argentina experienced during the recession was a reflection not solely of the currency board but also, in part, of the broader environment facing emerging markets. As such, it is unclear to what extent Argentina could have engineered substantial easing in its monetary stance in 1999–2000, even if it had abandoned the currency board. Already at this stage, an orderly exit from the currency board would have been very difficult to achieve, and would have required, at a minimum, significantly higher interest rates to curb capital outflows, suggesting little chance for monetary easing.

The stance of monetary policy during this period can also be viewed in relation to the behavior of money and credit aggregates: the growth of both broad money and credit to the economy in real terms decelerated substantially in 1998–2000, with real credit expansion becoming negative from mid-1999 through 2001 (Figure 12). Estimates suggest that this credit contraction was not a classic "credit crunch," but reflected in large part the negative effects on credit demand of the rising cost of funds and the shrinking economy (Box 11).

If the currency board did not exist, a nominal depreciation of the exchange rate could have helped offset the earlier shock to exports without the need for painful deflation. But a very substantial real depreciation would have been required to have an appreciable impact on growth in the short term due to low price responsiveness of exports (explained by the predominance of primary commodities) and the low share of external trade in the economy (Box 12). On the basis of the model described in Box 12, a 60 percent depreciation (broadly in line with the actual fall in Argentina's real effective exchange rate that occurred in 2002) would raise export volumes by a mere 5 percent in the short run, translating into a ½ percentage point contribution to real GDP growth. In reality, the growth of real exports of goods and services was close to zero in 2002 (on a national accounts basis), but has picked up since. In addition, as demonstrated by the events of 2002, a substantial depreciation would have boosted the peso value of Argentina's large foreign-currency liabilities. Even though the banking system itself held a long position in U.S. dollars, there would have been an adverse effect on banks through the increase in nonperforming loans, as borrowers with peso-denominated income streams would have started to default on dollar-denominated loans.[31] Together, these effects meant that any significant devaluation would have caused severe economic disruption.

A move to full dollarization would not have solved the dilemma either. The advantage of full dollarization over a currency board arrangement is that it implies an even stronger commitment to the exchange rate peg, since it is more difficult to reverse. This stronger commitment would generally be reflected in a lower exchange rate risk premium on interest rates. However, in Argentina, not much would have been gained from this credibility effect, as serious doubts about the currency board's sustainability did not surface until 2001. Although the spread between onshore dollar and peso interest rates occasionally reached as much as 3 percentage points, on average it was no more than 1½ to 2 percentage points prior to 2001—or about ½ percentage point greater than the average during 1996–97. More fundamentally though, no exchange rate regime could have alleviated the pressure on the government to restore debt sustainability. To the extent that dollarization would have simply perpetuated the existing inconsistencies, it would have been very unlikely to restore the confidence of either Argentine consumers and firms or foreign investors.

---

[31]For instance, it was estimated that a 50 percent devaluation would make half of all loans nonperforming.

Box 10. Monetary Conditions Indices for Argentina, Chile, and Mexico

A number of central banks have derived a monetary conditions index (MCIs) to help represent the stance of monetary policy. The basic premise of the MCI is that it captures the effects of changes in monetary policy on real output through the real interest rate and real exchange rate channels. The concept was initially developed at the Bank of Canada with weights of 3:1 attached to the real interest rate (lending rate) and the real exchange rate (CPI based), corresponding to the relative impact of these variables on the Canadian economy.[1] The relative weights approximate the ratio of exports and imports to output, measured in real terms. Since Argentina is considerably more closed to trade than Canada, a ratio of 9:1 was chosen for the relative weights for the Argentine MCI, broadly corresponding to its export ratio at 10 percent of GDP; for Chile and Mexico, relative weights of 2.5:1 were chosen, corresponding to export ratios for these two countries of about 30 percent of GDP. To smooth out movements in the real lending rate, a four-quarter moving average was used.

The MCI is presented relative to a baseline value when the monetary policy stance is neutral, defined as a point at which the economy is operating at its full potential. Since the Tequila crisis in 1995 severely disrupted these economies, it seems appropriate to consider a more recent period as the reference point. A standard Hodrick-Prescott filter revealed that each economy was operating at its full employment level in the first two quarters of 1997 and therefore this date was chosen as the reference point. This definition of a neutral policy stance is not without caveats, since a zero output gap does not necessarily imply that the real interest rate and the real exchange rate are at their long-term equilibrium levels. Moreover, to the extent that equilibrium rates change, movements in the MCI do not always correspond to shifts in the policy stance.

With the above caveats in mind, the top panel of the figure shows the close relationship between the MCI and the output gap in Argentina, with the tightening of the monetary policy stance in early 1995 associated with a sharp output decline later in the year. Similarly, the easing of monetary conditions over the period 1996–98 was associated with a booming economy, which was reversed in late 1998. Of course, it could be argued that the close relationship between the MCI and growth highlights the cost for Argentina of not being in control of monetary policy over this period.

The bottom panel shows a comparison of the monetary condition indices for Argentina, Chile, and Mexico, all presented relative to the common baseline. The chart shows that monetary conditions in Mexico were tight in late 1994, immediately prior to the devaluation, and that monetary conditions were similarly tight in Argentina in

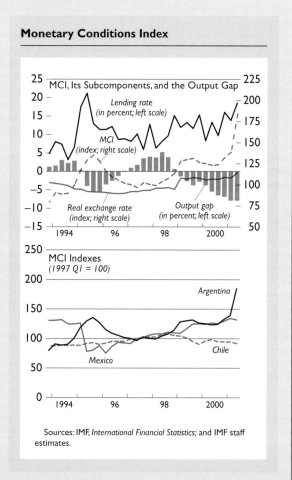

Monetary Conditions Index

MCI, Its Subcomponents, and the Output Gap

Lending rate (in percent; left scale)

MCI (index; right scale)

Real exchange rate (index; right scale)

Output gap (in percent; left scale)

MCI Indexes (1997 Q1 = 100)

Argentina

Mexico

Chile

Sources: IMF, *International Financial Statistics;* and IMF staff estimates.

[1] See Duguay (1994).

1995 following the Tequila crisis. However, by early 1997, monetary conditions were comparable in the three countries (by assumption), and these conditions did not diverge until early 1999 when monetary conditions in Argentina tightened considerably relative to Mexico, and especially Chile. By early 2000 the MCI in Mexico had risen to Argentina's level and it was not until early 2002 that Argentina diverged again significantly.

While it could be argued that Argentina should have adopted a floating exchange rate between 1996 and early 1998, it is clear that by late 1998 it was too late. Since monetary conditions in Mexico were comparable to those in Argentina by this time, it is unlikely that Argentina would have been able to adopt a looser monetary policy stance with a floating exchange rate. Indeed, based on history, it could have been expected that Argentina would have needed to keep interest rates high to avoid hyperinflation, although this is not what happened when the currency eventually floated.

Figure 12. Monetary Aggregates

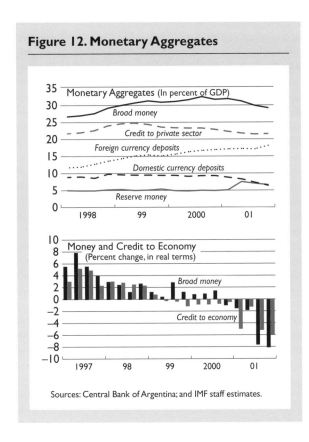

Sources: Central Bank of Argentina; and IMF staff estimates.

Summary

With the economy operating above potential in the first half of 1998, the initial downturn occurred as consumer confidence was sapped by external financial shocks and domestic political uncertainties, compounded by tighter monetary conditions and trade-related shocks; thereafter, the structural weaknesses came into play. The structure and low share of exports, arguably partly related to an appreciated real exchange rate, meant that the economy could not export its way out of recession; labor market rigidities limited the adjustment of real wages and contributed to a sharp increase in unemployment, which further eroded consumer confidence; debt dynamics ruled out expansionary fiscal policy; and while the scope for monetary policy in a small and financially open emerging-market economy is generally limited, the currency board regime precluded even a modest monetary stimulus.

Thus, once the depression was under way, there was no easy way out, as the authorities had no policy instruments that could have enabled them to stimulate the economy without compromising debt sustainability. Exiting the currency board via dollarization would not have solved this dilemma, while a float—which could have helped, in principle, to

---

Box 11. Was There a Credit Crunch?

A key question in assessing the various explanations for the economic downturn is whether there was a "credit crunch," perhaps because of the strictures on monetary easing implied by the currency board arrangement. To examine this possibility, a credit supply and credit demand function is estimated in a framework that allows explicitly for quantity rationing or disequilibrium in the credit markets. Credit supply is assumed to depend upon "lending capacity"—total banking system

assets (excluding repos) less cash-in-vault, deposits at the central bank, and equity—and upon the real lending rate. Credit demand is assumed to depend upon real GDP and on the real interest rate (both variables are instrumented using their lagged value, to reduce problems of endogeneity). The model is estimated using quarterly data over the period 1993–2001. The estimated parameters are of the expected signs and are generally statistically significant.

Demand and Supply of Credit to Private Sector

Parameter	Estimate	t-statistic	P-value
Demand function			
Constant	−0.6052	−0.11	[.913]
Real lending rate	−0.0125	−2.64	[.008]
Real GDP	0.9765	1.97	[.049]
Supply function			
Constant	9.6689	39.20	[.000]
Real lending capacity	0.0057	3.07	[.002]
Real lending rate	0.0006	0.03	[.975]
$\sigma 2$	0.0554	1.72	[.086]
$\sigma 1$	0.0541	2.51	[.012]
Number of obs	33		
Log likelihood	52.6		
Schwarz B.I.C.	−38.6		

Box 11 (*concluded*)

The top panel of the figure shows the estimated supply, demand, and actual credit to the private sector (in billions of 1993 pesos). The overall fit of the model may be gauged by how closely the minimum of supply and demand (at any instant) tracks the actual level of credit; the model seems to perform better in the second half of the sample.

Although actual credit falls precipitously beginning in early 1999, the model suggests that this mostly reflects falling credit demand rather than a contraction of credit supply—as such, there is little evidence of a quantity-rationing credit crunch. Indeed, as depicted in the lower panel, there seemed to be excess supply of credit as the economy contracted.

In part, however, credit demand was being choked off by rising real interest rates. The "counterfactual" excess credit demand line therefore shows how much excess demand there would have been had real lending interest rates remained at their 1994 level during the Tequila crisis, and at their 1998H1 level during the period 1998: H2-2001. Even in this counterfactual simulation, there is little evidence of excess demand for credit, belying the hypothesis that a "credit crunch" caused the recession.

Credits to Private Sector

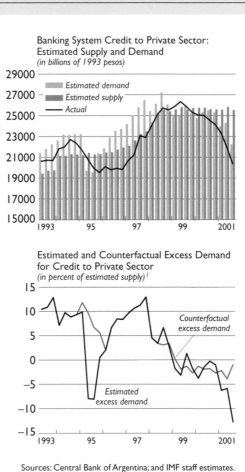

Sources: Central Bank of Argentina; and IMF staff estimates.
[1] Counterfactual is the excess demand that would have prevailed if, during 1995, the real lending interest rate had remained at its average 1994 level, and during 1998:H2–2001, the real lending rate had remained at its average 1998:H1 level.

Box 12. Empirical Estimates of the Effects of a Depreciation

Although the real exchange rate and the terms of trade had diverged sharply at the beginning of 1999, by mid-2000, the real exchange rate had stabilized and the terms of trade had improved. In volume terms, merchandise exports rose 14 percent between 1998 and 2000, and in value terms, despite the terms of trade deterioration, the average level of exports in 2000 was roughly the same as it had been in 1998. Many commentators have argued that Argentina should have devalued its currency and allowed it to float at this time to protect it against Brazil's devaluation. However, given the structure of Argentina's exports, in particular the large share of primary products, the price responsiveness of exports is low. Moreover, the small share of exports and imports in the economy implies that very substantial real depreciations would have been required to have an appreciable impact on growth.

To determine the magnitude of exchange rate adjustment that would be needed to stabilize the external debt in relation to GDP, a quarterly trade model for Argentina was estimated. The model consists of separate equations for the exports of commodities and other products, but treats all imports as one aggregate commodity. Since Argentina is a price taker for commodities, it takes the world commodity price as given. The volume of commodity exports is associated with the import volume of Argentina's trading partners and with the relative price of the world commodity price and foreign domestic deflators. The price of manufactured and services products is a weighted average of domestic unit labor costs and wholesale prices in Brazil (the main trading partner). The volume of manufactured goods is associated with the volume of Brazilian imports, and the price of Argentina's manufactured exports relative to Brazil's wholesale price index. Finally, import prices are associated with the world export price and import volumes are associated with domestic output and the relative price of imports versus that of domestic goods (measured by the GDP deflator). Since the volume and price terms are nonstationary variables, the analysis was conducted in first differences with a cointegrating relationship between the volume and price terms also included in the specifications.

The estimates revealed that real exports of commodities has a unit elasticity with respect to the world import volume and that the price effect is insignificant, implying that the demand for Argentine commodities does not react to price changes. Similarly, real exports of other

goods and services has a long-run unit elasticity with respect to Brazilian import volumes but in this case the price effect is significant, although the coefficient is significantly below unity signifying an inelastic demand for these products. The price of exports of goods and services (excluding commodities) is a weighted average of unit labor costs and the Brazilian wholesale price index in U.S. dollars with relative weights in the ratio of 1:3. The long-run elasticity of real imports with respect to domestic output is 2.76, considerably higher than the corresponding activity elasticity for exports. Finally, there is no identifiable price effect on the demand for imports.

The change in the balance on goods and services was calculated based on a 20 percent depreciation, and since Argentina is assumed to be a price taker for commodities, shocking the system by a depreciation of 20 percent has no effect on the world price of commodities. Moreover, since the world demand for commodities has not changed, revenues rise by a comparable amount. Taking advantage of the depreciation, exporters raise their domestic manufactures price by 6 percent, generating a 14 percent competitive improvement in the relative price of their products since competitor prices are now 20 percent higher. However, the demand for Argentine manufactures is price inelastic so that manufacturing revenues decline by 12 percent in foreign currency. On the imports side, foreign exporters lower their prices by 12 percent to maintain competitiveness generating an 8 percent increase in the import price in domestic currency. The demand for imports is inelastic so that import volumes are lowered only by 3 percent and expenditures in foreign currency are lowered by 15 percent.

Based on this model, a 60 percent depreciation (in line with the actual fall in Argentina's real effective exchange rate in 2002) would have improved the balance on goods and services by about US$24 billion (8½ percent of 1999 GDP), with the positive impact waning over time as the import price rises to fully reflect the depreciation. This improvement would have been sufficient to cover about half of Argentina's gross external financing needs, but would have resulted in a sharp increase in the debt-to-GDP ratio due to valuation effects. Indeed, the actual response in export volumes in 2002 was more sluggish, with an improvement in the trade and services balance equivalent to only half of the model's prediction, while the external debt ratio increased by about 80 percentage points of GDP.

---

jump-start the economy through a large depreciation—would have had major adverse repercussions via domestic balance sheets (including the public sector's large dollar-denominated liabilities). A possible alternative approach, at this stage, would have been a preemptive sovereign debt restructuring, which would have provided both sufficient liquidity and net present value relief, combined with a strategy to limit the adverse repercussions on banks' balance sheets. Taking this step could have also provided an opportunity to si-

multaneously exit from the currency board in favor of a more flexible arrangement that would have been more suitable for Argentina. However, at that stage, the authorities were understandably reluctant to adopt such a drastic approach, as a sovereign default was regarded as a last resort that should be taken only after all other policy options were exhausted. In these circumstances, the authorities hoped instead that an economic recovery would put a brake on the public debt dynamics as well as boost investors' confidence.

IV Crisis: 2001

As the situation continued to deteriorate, the authorities sought more international financing linked to strengthened policies. In January 2001, the IMF approved an augmentation of financing on the basis of a revamped program, centered on fiscal adjustment and accelerated structural reforms. The financing provided under Argentina's Stand-By Arrangement with the IMF was boosted to an equivalent of $14 billion, as part of a broader international support package of nearly $40 billion. About $3 billion of IMF support was made available immediately, and three additional tranches of about $1.3 billion were planned to be released during the remainder of 2001 in the context of subsequent reviews. The program sought to bolster the prospects for economic growth through gradual fiscal consolidation—an increase in the public sector primary surplus to 1½ percent of GDP from about ½ percent of GDP in 2000, with an overall deficit of about 3 percent of GDP—and various structural measures. The consolidation plan was formulated against the backdrop of a new fiscal pact with the provinces and envisaged improvements in tax enforcement. On the structural side, the program aimed at promoting private investment and competition in domestic markets through, among other things, elimination of tax disincentives, continued implementation of already approved labor market reforms, and deregulation of key sectors—but did not include structural performance criteria or benchmarks to this effect. On the basis of these measures and the anticipated positive confidence effects, real GDP was assumed to grow by 2½ percent, and the public sector debt ratio was projected to increase only modestly to 52½ percent of GDP.

The attempts at strengthening the public finances failed, however, to break the cycle of rising interest rates, falling growth, and fiscal underperformance. Financial markets initially responded positively to the revised program, but already by mid-February it became evident that the fiscal deficit was about to exceed the agreed ceiling for the first quarter. Moreover, following the resignation of the finance minister, his successor was forced out of office in less than two weeks as his planned budgetary cuts and reform measures failed to find the necessary political backing. Doubts about the sustainability of the public debt dynamics and the currency board arrangement resurfaced quickly, evidenced by rising spreads and sizable deposit outflows.

Within the fixed exchange rate regime, the authorities undertook a number of measures aimed at improving competitiveness, with little effect other than to erode confidence and widen spreads further.[32] The majority of these measures were adopted without prior consultation with the IMF. In particular, the government tried to engineer an increase in export competitiveness.[33] In April 2001, a "convergence factor" for foreign trade in nonenergy goods was introduced under which exporters received a reimbursement, and importers paid a tax, equivalent to the difference between the exchange rate pegged to the U.S. dollar and that on a corresponding equally weighted euro-U.S. dollar basket.[34] This was, in essence, a crypto-devaluation; such tinkering with the currency board arrangement further harmed confidence. The spread between peso- and U.S. dollar-denominated interest rates, which had started the year at less than 1 percentage point, increased to 9 percentage points in April. The spread increased further, to almost 16 percentage points, in mid-year, when the central bank charter was modified to allow greater room for liquidity injections, reducing the required currency backing under the Convertibility Law.

---

[32]Appendix II provides a list of the main policy measures undertaken in 2001–2002.

[33]In addition, several "competitiveness plans" were launched to increase profitability in the sectors most affected by the recession. These were estimated to cost ½ percent of GDP in revenues, but they proved largely ineffective, and complicated tax administration considerably. Most—though not all—were abandoned later in the year.

[34]The authorities also announced that the peso would be repegged to an equally weighted basket of the dollar and the euro, once the euro had reached parity with the dollar (which, however, did not take place prior to the collapse of the currency board arrangement). Indeed, this strategy would have likely worsened competitiveness problems, to the extent that the peso would have been partially repegged from a currency on a depreciating trend (the U.S. dollar) to one on an appreciating trend (the euro).

These various efforts were largely ineffective in stabilizing output, which fell at an annual rate of about 4 percent in each of the second and third quarters of 2001. As it became increasingly clear that Argentina would be unable to grow out of its debt problem, the authorities made further, unsuccessful attempts to stabilize the public debt dynamics, including through a debt swap. The debt swap was a voluntary, market-based debt exchange operation completed in June 2001. It bought some temporary breathing space, but at a high cost in terms of the public sector's longer-term solvency. Against market expectations that some $18 billion to $24 billion of face value of bonds would be swapped, the operation swapped $29.5 billion—nearly the full amount of the offers received ($32.8 billion). Although the swap reduced debt service obligations falling due in 2001–2005 by some $12.6 billion, the implicit interest rate on the operation—the discount rate that equalizes the present value of pre- and post-swap debt-service payments—was more than 17 percent per year. This far exceeded the expected growth rate of the economy (a natural benchmark for assessing long-term solvency) and contributed further to concerns about the solvency of the public sector.[35]

As the government ran out of funding options, the currency board arrangement, with its stricture against money financing of the deficit, could be maintained only with a zero cash deficit—or indeed a surplus, as creditors became unwilling even to roll over maturing debt. A zero-deficit law was passed, aimed at regaining control of the public debt dynamics through across-the-board cuts in primary spending. But by the time the law was approved by Congress at the end of July, spreads between peso- and U.S. dollar-denominated interest rates had reached 1,500–2,000 basis points, rendering the option of a zero deficit both increasingly unlikely and ineffective in maintaining the currency board. Indeed, the resumption, in July, of large-scale withdrawals of deposits from Argentine banks was perhaps the clearest sign of the system's impending collapse absent any dramatic changes in economic policies or circumstances. In any event, delays in reaching agreement on a revised revenue-sharing arrangement with the provinces meant that the rule was never fully implemented.

At this stage, serious consideration should already have been given to an involuntary debt restructuring, with reduction in the present value of the debt, accompanied by an exit from the currency board arrangement. With GDP falling at an annual rate of 4 percent and spreads reaching 1,000 basis points,

preventing a further rise in the debt ratio would have required an implausibly large primary surplus of about 8 percent of GDP. Thus, by this point, barring some extraordinarily favorable shock, the debt dynamics were clearly unsustainable and stronger consideration should have been given to a debt restructuring—involving short-term liquidity relief as well as a significant reduction in the present value of public debt—combined with a strategy to limit the repercussions of such a step for the banking system. While the public banks, which, by mid-2001, held around one-quarter of their assets in the form of government bonds, were especially vulnerable, it was estimated that a major haircut on the value of government debt would do substantial damage to the overall banking system's capital, as well as creating serious liquidity problems, given banks' reliance on government securities for meeting liquidity requirements.[36]

Faced with either "pulling the plug" and implicitly forcing a radical redesign of policies, or further augmenting its financial support to Argentina in tandem with strengthened policies under the existing framework, the IMF decided in favor of the latter. Despite concerns about the lack of political support for the measures that would be needed to achieve the zero-deficit target, the IMF agreed in early September of 2001 to support the new program and to disburse $5 billion immediately (pledging another $3 billion in support of prospective debt restructuring). This disbursement, which was aimed at restoring market confidence, doubled the IMF's existing exposure to Argentina (or nearly quadrupled it over a period of only nine months). The desired recovery of confidence, however, proved elusive—with legislative elections in mid-October further weakening the government's political support—and neither the planned fiscal improvement nor the envisaged rebound in economic activity materialized: GDP dropped by $4\frac{1}{2}$ percent in 2001; the primary and overall fiscal positions ended up 3 percentage points of GDP weaker than anticipated (in September); and the debt-to-GDP ratio rose above 60 percent.

In November, the authorities made an additional effort to restructure the public debt, involving the exchange of $41 billion federal and $10 billion provincial peso- and U.S. dollar-denominated bonds for domestic guaranteed loans. These carried a maximum interest rate of 7 percent, a grace period for interest until April 2002, and a three-year maturity extension of bonds falling due by 2010. Phase I of the operation was directed at domestic creditors; participation included $13 billion from domestic banks on their

---

[35]In present value terms, using a discount rate of 5 percent per year (approximating the potential growth rate of nominal GDP), for instance, the operation entailed Argentina saving $12.6 billion debt service obligations in 2001–05 at the cost of $22.1 billion.

[36]It was estimated that a hypothetical 70 percent haircut on public debt would be sufficient to wipe out the entire capital of the banking system.

own account, $11 billion on behalf of their clients, and $17 billion from pension funds. Phase II of the debt restructuring—aimed at nonresidents (and those who did not participate in the first phase more generally)—was never undertaken.

The crisis broke with a run of private sector deposits, which fell by more than $3.6 billion (6 percent of the deposit base) during November 28–30. The authorities responded with a wide range of controls on banking and foreign exchange transactions. These included a weekly limit of 250 pesos on withdrawals from individual bank accounts (*el corralito*), a prohibition on banks from granting loans in pesos, and foreign exchange restrictions on travel and transfers abroad. The ensuing riots and protests—in which more than 20 demonstrators died—forced the resignation of President Fernando de La Rua on December 20.

By the end of 2001, both the economy and the public finances were in deep crisis. In December, economic activity collapsed, with industrial production falling by 18 percent (year-on-year), construction by 36 percent, and imports by more than 50 percent. Tax revenues plummeted 17 percent (year-on-year) in the final quarter of 2001 (in December, tax collections fell by almost 30 percent, year-on-year), and despite across-the-board spending cuts, the federal government ran an overall deficit of 4½ percent of GDP in 2001 against a (revised) program target of 2½ percent. Provincial finances also deteriorated, with the deficit widening to 2 percent of GDP against a program target of 1 percent. Moreover, out of 17 billion pesos of federal transfers to the provinces, about 1 billion pesos were in the form of federal guarantees of provincial treasury bills (*lecops*), while the provincial governments issued about 1.6 billion pesos in provincial bills (quasi-monies) to pay wages and suppliers, some of which were acceptable by the federal government in lieu of tax payments. On December 23, the new President Adolfo Rodríguez Saá declared the intention to default on government debt (except on debt that had been subject to the phase I restructuring) and to call presidential elections within 60 days.

V   Aftermath: 2002

On January 3, 2002, President Eduardo Duhalde—the fifth president in three weeks—confirmed the debt moratorium (as well as the intention to negotiate with private creditors) and announced the end of the convertibility regime. Three days later, Congress effectively replaced the convertibility regime with a dual exchange rate system based on an official exchange rate of 1.4 pesos per U.S. dollar for public sector and most trade-related transactions (except luxury imports); all other transactions would take place at prevailing market rates.[37] At the same time, the monthly deposit withdrawal limit was raised to 1,500 pesos (from its previous limit of 1,000 pesos), coupled with the freezing of term-deposits (*corralon*), and it was decided to keep dollar deposits frozen until at least 2003. To dampen inflationary pressures, prices of privatized utilities (gas, electricity, telephones, and water) were frozen indefinitely. Congress also approved an emergency law that severely curtailed creditors' rights.

While the incoming government faced enormous challenges, many of the initial measures—which were undertaken without consulting the IMF—not only failed to stabilize the situation but complicated any eventual resolution of the crisis (See Appendix II). Especially damaging was the government's announcement on February 3 that banks' assets and liabilities would be subject to asymmetric "pesoization." Under this scheme, the existing stock of banks' dollar-denominated assets and liabilities would be converted at the rate of 1 peso to the U.S. dollar for loans to the private sector and 1.4 pesos to the U.S. dollar for loans to the public sector and for U.S. dollar deposits, which were also indexed to inflation. The measure was intended to protect firms and households with foreign-currency-denominated debt, but it merely shifted the burden of the devaluation to the banking system—and ultimately to the taxpayer as banks would need to be issued compensation bonds.[38] The main effect of the measure was to deepen financial disintermediation, curtailing the supply of fresh credit—including working capital—that banks were able to provide and that would be critical in any eventual recovery.

The difficulties of the banking sector were exacerbated by the asymmetric price indexation of bank balance sheets and continued withdrawal of term deposits because of court-ordered injunctions (*amparos*), which required banks to pay out U.S. dollar-denominated deposits at the prevailing market exchange rate (rather than the 1.40 pesos per U.S. dollar at which they were *pesoized* and indexed).

The immediate macroeconomic consequences of the crisis were severe. Real GDP fell by about 11 percent in 2002, bringing the cumulative decline since 1998 to almost 20 percent; and the unemployment rate rose above 20 percent. Inflation peaked at a monthly rate of about 10 percent in April, driven by liquidity provision from the central bank to banks experiencing deposit withdrawals, but then declined, averaging around 40 percent for the year as a whole. On a cash basis, the consolidated public sector primary balance moved into a surplus of ½ percent of GDP, but the overall deficit rose to 10½ percent of GDP. Reflecting the effects of the exchange rate depreciation on foreign-currency-denominated debt, the issuance of debt to compensate banks for the asymmetric *pesoization,* and the accumulation of arrears, the public debt ratio more than doubled from 63 percent of GDP at end-2001 to about 135 percent of GDP at end-2002.

---

[37]On January 11, export surrender requirements were introduced and transfers of funds abroad were blocked unless they related to certified foreign trade transactions or were explicitly authorized by the central bank. On February 11, the dual exchange rate system was abolished and the market opened for the first time under a unified regime; the exchange rate depreciated to 1.8 pesos per U.S. dollar.

[38]The government eventually announced the issuance of compensation bonds amounting to about 9 billion.

VI   Role of the IMF

In light of the gravity of the crisis that unfolded while the country was engaged in a succession of IMF-supported programs it is not surprising that the IMF has come under harsh criticism for its involvement in Argentina. Indeed, with hindsight, the IMF—like most other observers—overestimated Argentina's growth potential and underestimated its vulnerabilities. These misjudgments resulted in IMF-supported programs that were insufficiently ambitious and excessively accommodative of slippages, particularly through 1998 when the economy was booming. Although the IMF warned the authorities at least by early 1998 about the country's growing vulnerabilities and the need for further fiscal adjustment and structural reform, the institution continued to provide its support on the basis of a policy package that was ultimately inadequate.

The most glaring omission was in the fiscal area, where the IMF condoned repeated slippages of debt and deficit targets. The private financial community was willing to finance the growing borrowing requirement associated with this fiscal deterioration, until late 2000. Indeed, the federal government underperformed on its fiscal targets in every single year since 1994 (Figure 13).[39] While part of the underperformance, particularly after 1998, was the result of the weaker-than-expected growth, fiscal targets were frequently missed even on cyclically adjusted terms. The IMF reacted to these slippages by pressing for some fiscal correction in the following year, but part of the previous underperformance was effectively accommodated, while the time frame for restoring a fiscal surplus was repeatedly pushed out into the medium term on the basis of what turned out to be overly optimistic growth assumptions.

In retrospect, it is also clear that the IMF-supported programs had insufficient structural content and conditionality, given that the currency board arrangement, together with the relatively small share of exports in the economy, put a premium on the flexibility and resilience of the domestic economy. The 1992–95 arrangement under the Extended Fund Facility, for instance, included only two structural

benchmarks—on the implementation of tax reforms (which was undertaken) and of social security reform (which was not undertaken until 1994). With regard to the supply side, the IMF's main focus was on labor market reform, but it attached no conditionality to its implementation. Likewise, in the first and second reviews of the 1996 Stand-By Arrangement, the IMF encouraged the authorities to implement the labor market reforms contained in the 1996 draft bill, but there was no structural conditionality attached. When the proposed reforms became much weaker, the IMF did little beyond express concern. Labor market reform was one of the pillars of the new arrangement under the Extended Fund Facility in early 1998, but program conditionality was introduced only in the form of (nonbinding) structural benchmarks—and when the authorities did not deliver on their original intentions, the IMF did not press the issue. In later reviews, comments on the labor market were largely absent, overtaken by other pressing concerns. Even less attention was paid to other standard issues that, arguably, were equally important to the flexibility of the economy—notably, those related to trade policy and governance. The structural aspects of fiscal policy, including tax administration and fiscal federal issues, were also given insufficient emphasis.

It is debatable whether greater structural conditionality—or stricter enforcement—would have succeeded in ensuring that structural reforms would be undertaken, given that political consensus and ownership were lacking. Nevertheless, condionality could have interrupted IMF support if ownership was lacking, which would have been less damaging to the IMF's credibility, including its implicit "seal of approval" when the arrangement was precautionary.

While the decision to establish and maintain the currency board arrangement was the authorities' and commanded broad popular support, the IMF could have questioned more forcefully the appropriateness of the arrangement and of the associated policy mix. The IMF was initially skeptical about the adoption of the currency board, but this view changed as the arrangement demonstrated its success in bringing down inflation where other approaches had failed.

---

[39]Program reviews were nevertheless completed, as performance criteria were either met on the basis of adjusters or waived.

Figure 13. Fiscal Performance Under IMF-Supported Programs

(In percent of GDP, unless otherwise indicated)

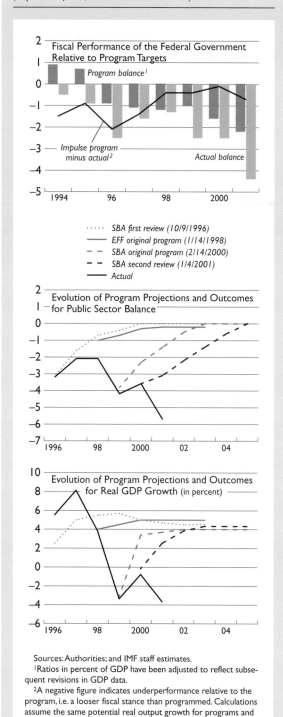

Sources: Authorities; and IMF staff estimates.

[1]Ratios in percent of GDP have been adjusted to reflect subsequent revisions in GDP data.

[2]A negative figure indicates underperformance relative to the program, i.e. a looser fiscal stance than programmed. Calculations assume the same potential real output growth for programs and actual outcomes (consistent with figures in Table 1).

Thereafter, the IMF showed considerable deference to the authorities' choice of exchange rate regime, despite some doubts about its viability and its consistency with other policies. This raises the question of whether this deference was appropriate or whether the IMF should have made its support conditional on a timely exit. A timely exit from the currency board would have been very difficult, given the popularity of the arrangement. Moreover, as noted earlier, a series of crises in other emerging market countries meant that there were relatively few opportunities for a graceful exit, without being caught up in the turbulence in international capital markets. But with the currency board in place, it was all the more important to ensure that other economic policies be consistent with it. At the very least, the IMF should have insisted on greater prudence regarding the public debt dynamics during the boom years, since the currency board regime ruled out both discretionary monetary policy for stabilization purposes and money financing of the deficit when the government ran into funding difficulties.

The IMF's decision to continue its support to Argentina during the pre-crisis period, including through its endorsement of policies under the precautionary arrangement, despite repeated policy slippages, must be evaluated in the context of the available alternatives. There was an evident fear among the IMF's shareholders, and the international community at large, that policies would quickly deteriorate in the absence of IMF oversight. Faced with this alternative, and realizing the limited leverage to bring about substantial policy improvements, the program, certainly through 1999, was seen as providing a degree of policy discipline. Moreover, since the arrangement was precautionary until the end of 1999, IMF exposure was diminishing, implying a low cost and higher potential benefits from continued involvement. These strategic considerations created strong momentum for continued program support, even though the risks became increasingly clear, as recorded in internal documents and program reports.

When the economy slid into recession, the IMF faced a somewhat different and more serious dilemma. In terms of policy advice, fiscal easing in support of growth was not a viable option given the exploding debt dynamics, while tightening would exacerbate the downturn. In hindsight, the most viable option would appear to have been an early debt restructuring involving a significant present value reduction, combined with the abandonment of the currency board. However, the authorities were unwilling even to consider the possibility of an exit: neither the government nor the public were prepared to take such a drastic course until it was forced upon them by events. During this time, the authorities could not but be aware that the IMF was loath to withdraw its support for fear of adverse consequences. "Pulling the plug" at this stage would almost surely have precipitated a crisis that both the government and the IMF still hoped to avoid. Moreover, there were concerns that, in the absence of a framework for orderly debt restructuring, a default would lead to chaos. In the end, the IMF chose to continue to provide financing in the hope that the government would deliver on its commitments and that confidence and growth

would return—in effect, allowing the authorities to "gamble for redemption." While this strategy— when adopted in early 2001—might have succeeded in a more favorable external and political environment, by mid-2001 the chances of success had become minimal. At this stage, the provision of significant new financing only postponed the inevitable and, by raising the debt burden, also meant that the costs of the eventual collapse were all the greater.

VII   Conclusions

To a striking degree, Argentina's crisis involved vulnerabilities that were already present or indeed were building up during the boom years of the 1990s—when the country was widely viewed as a star performer. The key elements of vulnerability were the public debt dynamics, the constraint on monetary policy imposed by the currency board, and weaknesses on the structural side. There was little sense of urgency to address these vulnerabilities at that time, given the widespread eagerness to interpret the boom as the onset of an era of permanently higher growth founded on structural reforms and sound macroeconomic policies.

Once the economic slump set in, the vulnerabilities surfaced. As the economy remained depressed, the debt dynamics became explosive. The fiscal adjustment necessary to stabilize the debt ratio was not forthcoming and eventually the required primary surplus became implausibly large, particularly in relation to the political system's ability to deliver. On the other hand, the debt dynamics constrained the authorities' ability to stimulate the economy, and the potential for export-led growth was limited by structural weaknesses and unfavorable external conditions. By 2001, almost no strategy would have succeeded without a sovereign debt restructuring that reduced the present value of Argentina's public debt burden.

The currency board turned from being a source of policy credibility to a handicap. On the one hand, the currency board was relatively successful in containing the adverse effects of financial market contagion from the Russian default. In addition, while Argentina lost competitiveness under the currency board following the Brazilian devaluation and the appreciation of the U.S. dollar, the direct impact on the economy was muted by exports' limited role in the economy. On the other hand, the currency board may have suppressed a more rapid expansion of exports after trade was liberalized and did constrain monetary policy when the economy slid into recession. In addition, competitiveness was one of the concerns behind the widening spreads on Argentina's sovereign bonds, particularly since under the fixed exchange rate regime, real exchange rate adjustments required deflation of nominal wages and prices, which was not only difficult to achieve but also contributed to weakening economic activity. Finally, by lending credibility to the exchange rate peg, the currency board arrangement allowed Argentina's public sector to continue borrowing excessively in international capital markets, thereby raising the cost of the eventual collapse. Indeed, within the above concerns, the public sector's excessive debt creation—and thus, the inconsistency of fiscal policy with the requirements of a "money dominant" regime—was arguably the single most important factor behind Argentina's demise.

While the crisis itself was the result of economic forces that were difficult to reverse in the context of Argentina's existing vulnerabilities, it was exacerbated by a series of policy mistakes. Some key steps during 2001 included actions to tinker with the currency board, which undermined confidence but provided no additional room for maneuver, while voluntary debt swaps substantially increased the present value of debt service. The measures surrounding the collapse of the currency board and public debt default—notably the capital controls, the *corralito* and *corralon,* and the asymmetrical *pesoization* and *indexation*—exacerbated the macroeconomic consequences of the crisis and complicated its resolution.

Looking forward, the country faces enormous challenges not only in restoring macroeconomic stability but also in re-establishing the pre-eminence of contracts, property rights, and economic security that has been damaged by the government's default on its debt and abandonment of its convertibility commitment. Damage both to the balance sheets and to the credibility of the banking system also needs to be repaired. While the devaluation has addressed immediate concerns about competitiveness, one troubling aspect of the performance of the Argentine economy was that, even during its boom years, 1991–98, unemployment remained persistently high, underscoring the need for reforms of the labor market and for other improvements in economic institutions and structures that foster a more dynamic private sector. On the macroeconomic policy front, Argentina will first need to develop and implement a coherent monetary policy framework. In terms of the public finances, even with a major debt restructuring, substantial primary surpluses will be required to service the massive increase in public sector liabilities (including those related to the recapitalization of the banking system). More generally, there needs to be a fundamental re-thinking of the role of the state—not least, in the relations between the federal government and the provinces and in the size and cost of the civil service—if expenditure is to be commensurate with revenues.

Lessons for Crisis Prevention and Management

Argentina's story underscores many of the lessons that we have learned from previous crises. It serves as another illustration of the complex dynamic interactions among various sources of vulnerability that crises frequently involve, and, in view of these interactions, of how difficult it is to resolve a crisis once it starts. Argentina is also a reminder that very severe vulnerabilities can build up in countries that are widely viewed as "star performers." The fact that most of the usual indicators of impending difficulties did not look alarming until the situation had deteriorated to the point that there was no good exit is indeed disconcerting. These considerations emphasize that there remains considerable work to do on crisis anticipation and prevention.

Growth projections were a central symptom of the failure of most actors—including the authorities, the IMF, and market participants—to identify the vulnerabilities that were building up during the boom years of the 1990s. During that period, Argentina's growth projections were based on what was, in hindsight, an overly favorable reading of the benefits of the structural reforms that had taken place and prospects that further reforms would be implemented. This experience calls for a careful and critical assessment of the links between structural reforms and growth, both in the context of work on individual countries and in cross-country analysis. But at the same time, projecting growth after a structural change inevitably involves an element of judgment, and in view of the irreducible uncertainties, it is essential to stress-test projections with regard to plausible alternatives.

The Argentine crisis calls for a new focus on sovereign debt and the debt dynamics, both with regard to crisis prevention and resolution. It is striking that, when Argentina's debt started on the path of no return, its level (as a share of GDP) was in a range not previously viewed as alarming. This experience clearly calls for a more cautious assessment of debt levels, in view of a careful consideration of the scope

for adjustment in the event of adverse circumstances. In Argentina's case, the "danger level" of debt needed to be viewed, in particular, in the light of the exchange rate regime, the comparatively small share of exports and their concentration, the political and administrative factors that limited the room for maneuver on the fiscal side, the country's large size in emerging markets worldwide, and the relative lack of flexibility of its labor and product markets. The need for a systematic and disciplined analysis of debt sustainability, illustrated by the Argentine experience, has motivated recent IMF work in this area,[40] and has influenced decisions on exceptional access and prolonged use of IMF resources, in an attempt to strike the right balance between supporting a member experiencing difficulties and safeguarding IMF resources.[41]

With regard to crisis resolution, the Argentine crisis illustrates the importance of timely debt restructuring in cases in which the debt dynamics have become irreversible. Once a debt restructuring has become unavoidable, measures to delay it are likely to raise the costs of the crisis and further complicate its resolution. At the same time, the crisis also illustrates the pervasive effects of a default on the financial system and macroeconomic policies—making the exchange rate regime unviable and compromising an otherwise healthy financial system. The experience suggests that it would be desirable, if it is possible, to find a more orderly approach to debt restructuring. This was an important initial motivation for the IMF's work on the Sovereign Debt Restructuring Mechanism (SDRM). The underlying problem remains: the Argentine experience highlights the need to find better ways of anticipating and resolving debt crises.

The Argentine crisis also entails important lessons for exchange rate regimes. We would not conclude that Argentina's currency board was a mistake from the start: on the contrary, the currency board was critical in taming hyperinflation when many other approaches had failed. Particularly given this early success, it would have been an extremely difficult political decision to exit without a crisis. But a currency board puts much more stringent demands than other regimes on fiscal and financial policies, as well as on the flexibility of trade and the labor market. Given the structure of the Argentine economy, a peg

---

[40]See IMF (2002a).

[41]The new exceptional access framework requires, among other things, a rigorous analysis of debt sustainability and good prospects of the member regaining access to private capital markets within the time IMF resources would be outstanding. On prolonged use, the IMF's Executive Board concluded that the IMF should apply consistently the existing policies on financing for countries with slow progress toward external viability, including that access for such countries should continue to be guided by the need to reduce their outstanding use of IMF resources over time.

to the U.S. dollar was arguably not an ideal arrangement once inflation was successfully reduced to single digits. Indeed, to the extent that the currency board arrangement encouraged the buildup of balance sheet mismatches, an earlier exit (e.g., in 1992–94 or in 1996–97) would have been preferable. Such an exit, had it been undertaken sooner, would not have been painless, but it would likely have been less painful than what actually occurred. This illustrates the importance of an appropriate macroeconomic policy mix and, more specifically, an exchange-rate regime that fits a country's economic and political realities. A currency board can have specific temporary advantages, irrespective of a country's economic structures—such as achieving disinflation—but if its long-term benefits are questionable, it is important to exit the arrangement in time before market pressures make it untenable.

More generally, the Argentine experience points to the limits in the ability of an exchange rate arrangement—even when strongly endorsed by the authorities and the public—to discipline other aspects of economic policy in a way that ensures stability. This experience is also a reminder that "hard pegs" are not as hard as is often supposed: *in extremis,* a government can unwind a currency board, albeit at considerable cost to the country. The forced redenomination of bank assets and liabilities also serves as a reminder that there are limits to the extent to which a peg can be durably hardened through formal dollarization. Moreover, to the extent that a hard peg does secure credibility, this can be a mixed blessing: the high credibility of Argentina's currency board through 2000 helped enable the country to borrow from the capital markets at spreads that did not fully reflect the risks. This temporarily insulated the country from adverse market reactions to unsustainable policies, and thus ultimately allowed a much bigger disaster to materialize.

Lessons for the IMF

The occurrence and severity of the Argentine crisis have been particularly disturbing to the IMF given its extensive engagement for many years beforehand. Of course, key policy decisions on the exchange rate regime and the lack of supportive fiscal and structural policies were the authorities', and the IMF expressed concerns over the vulnerability of the situation, as early as 1998. Moreover, in the run-up to the crisis, the authorities took damaging steps, either without consulting the IMF or against the IMF's advice. But the IMF's experience in Argentina does call for some fresh thinking about its role, both in normal times and in the context of a crisis. Several of these lessons—like the more general lessons on the eco-

nomics of crises just summarized—are starting to be reflected in the IMF's work.[42]

The Argentine crisis reflects shortcomings in IMF surveillance to identify early on the vulnerabilities that emerged during the boom period, and in bringing about needed changes once these vulnerabilities became apparent. The experience highlights the risk that, in a program country, where attention is focused on implementation of the program, it is easy to lose sight of the need for a fresh and critical assessment of the overall direction of policies. In particular, the IMF's macroeconomic projections, like those of the authorities and market participants, extrapolated the favorable growth results of the 1990s and did not adequately scrutinize the basis for this growth. There was not sufficient attention paid to the fact that the structural reforms that were seen as critical to growth had largely stalled. Fiscal policy assessments were not based on an adequate appraisal of the risks to debt sustainability in the event of a slowdown in growth. Moreover, the exchange rate assessments in Argentina did not stress the need for a timely exit; instead, the IMF accepted the authorities' refusal to discuss a possible change in the status quo until a change was forced by the markets. Such assessments should be more proactive, asking the tough questions and recommending needed changes in noncrisis times. This experience is a significant motivation for recent initiatives to strengthen the IMF's surveillance in program countries by ensuring a fresh look at the economic issues.[43]

A second area in which the Argentine experience has had an important impact is with regard to the decision to commit IMF resources. During the years of deepening depression, as it became increasingly clear that the situation was deteriorating in several dimensions, the IMF nonetheless endeavored to help the country by providing financing and its accompanying "seal of approval." This pattern continued through September 2001, when the IMF approved one last significant tranche of financing despite considerable doubts about the prospects for success, and despite the authorities' steps taken against the IMF's advice in the preceding months. The IMF's decision was understandable in light of the high and immediate costs of withdrawing support, but the low probability of success should have outweighed these concerns. This experience raises difficult questions about how the IMF—and the international community more generally—can strike the right balance between supporting a member country experiencing difficulties without financing and implicitly perpetuating policies that are doomed to fail. Following the

---

[42]An extensive review of the IMF's role in Argentina was prepared by the Independent Evaluation Office subsequent to this report, and was issued in 2004.

[43]See IMF (2002b).

collapse of the currency board, the IMF took a more cautious approach by waiting for the authorities to assemble a viable policy package rather than rushing to provide new financing.

The experience raises more general questions about the IMF's use of its "seal of approval." If the IMF had chosen to withdraw its financial support, the direct financing effects would have been limited, as the institution's financial exposure—at least until September 2001—covered a relatively small portion of Argentina's total borrowing requirements. The main consequences would have been the adverse impact on market sentiment and negative political repercussions that would have likely been felt far beyond Argentina. In balancing these considerations, the IMF decided to continue providing its support, despite serious concerns over fiscal and external sustainability. Such attempts to make strategic use of the "seal of approval" ultimately devalue that signal and compromise the IMF's credibility more generally. The limits to the IMF's involvement should be based on the underlying quality of policies, not on the perceived cost of withdrawing support. That said, the IMF's decision to continue or withdraw its support to a member country in particular circumstances is always made under uncertainty, and more likely than not the IMF will continue to make occasional judgment errors and take decisions that will prove wrong *ex post*.

An important consideration that has to guide the IMF's decision-making process and that was clearly underscored by the Argentine experience is that, in a situation in which the debt dynamics are clearly unsustainable, the IMF should not provide its financing. To the extent that such financing helps stave off a needed debt restructuring, it only compounds the ultimate cost of such a restructuring. This consideration has led the IMF to search for better ways of facilitating debt restructuring in cases in which it is a necessary element in the policy package. The initial proposal for an SDRM, which was intended to tackle this problem, has not been implemented due to insufficient international support, although there has been progress with other approaches, including the promotion of collective action clauses (CACs) in sovereign bonds and a code of conduct. The problem the SDRM was meant to address has not gone away, and there remains a need for further work to strengthen the capacity for sovereign debt restructuring within the present legal framework.

The Argentine experience also provides lessons for conditionality and ownership. First, it is a reminder that the injunction in the IMF's 2002 Conditionality Guidelines to focus on what is critical to achieve macroeconomic objectives is a positive as well as a negative one. In Argentina, the programs did not include certain structural reforms—notably involving trade and labor markets—that, at least in hindsight, were indeed critical to achieving sustainability and addressing key vulnerabilities. Moreover, even those structural measures that were included were often not implemented.

The Argentine experience also highlights the fact that, while ownership of policies is important, it is not sufficient to guarantee their viability. Arguably, in Argentina there was strong ownership for an inconsistent set of policies—with wide popular support in particular for the currency board but not for the fiscal policies needed to support it. Ensuring that policies are both nationally owned and viable is a very complex challenge that the IMF and the country authorities need to face.

Appendix I Argentina's Potential Output Growth

As a result of Argentina's strong growth performance following the stabilization at the beginning of the 1990s, and its recovery from the Tequila crisis, by mid-decade it was commonly assumed that Argentina's potential output growth was in the range of 4½ to 5 percent per year. At least in retrospect, however, there are reasons to believe that this represented a significant overestimate of potential output growth.

Potential output growth is the growth rate of the economy at which, in the absence of monetary impulses, there should be no inflationary pressures. Conceptually, potential output growth need not be constant. Indeed, to the extent that Argentina's structural reforms (including deregulation, privatization, and labor market reforms) in the early part of the decade gave a boost to the *level* of potential output, potential output growth would surge initially but then return toward its longer-run rate—especially as structural reforms began to fizzle and in, some instances, to be reversed.

One approach to estimating potential output growth is to fit a smoothing filter to actual real GDP. This allows for some variation in the growth rate of potential output. Given the structural changes of the economy, however, the key question concerns the period over which the filter should be applied. Quarterly (seasonally adjusted) national accounts data are available from 1993, and given that growth in 1991–92 was probably driven by a rebound from the collapse during the hyperinflation, 1993 provides a convenient starting point. More tricky is the choice of the end-point. Figure 14 shows two possible choices, ending the sample period in 1999:Q4 (labeled A) or 2000:Q4 (labeled B); beyond these terminal dates, potential output growth is extrapolated using the final quarter's growth rate.[44]

---

[44]By 2001, the economy is clearly in collapse and including 2001 in the estimation sample leads to a downward bias of potential output over the entire period.

Figure 14. Potential Output and Output Gap

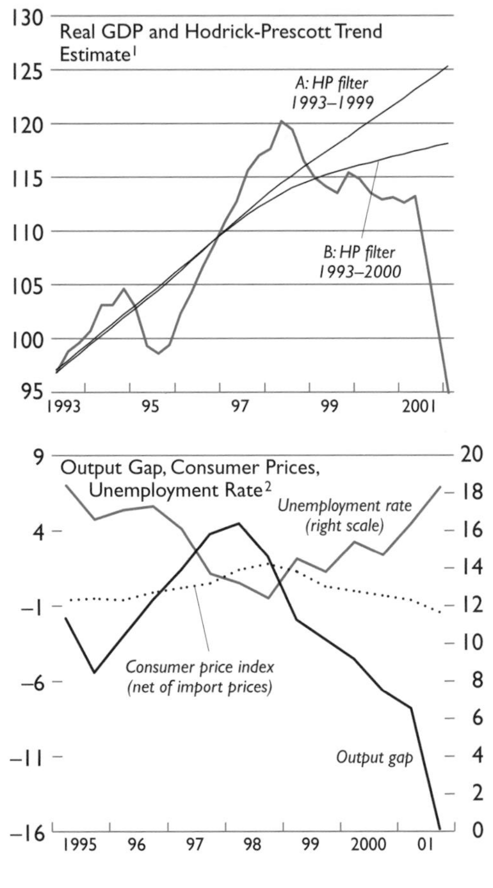

[1]A Hodrick-Prescott filter is applied to the period 1993:1–1999:4 (Trend A) or 1993:1–2000:4 (Trend B); potential output thereafter is extrapolated using the last quarter's growth rate.

[2]Output gap implied by Trend A; positive output gap indicates actual output above estimated potential output.

Using Trend A, output was on average 2 percent above potential in 1997 and, on average, almost 3½ percent above potential in 1998. The growth slowdown brought the economy to 2½ percent below potential in 1999, 5½ percent below potential by 2000, and almost 12 percent below potential by 2001. Using Trend B, output was almost 4½ percent above potential in 1998, close to its natural level in 1999, 2½ percent below potential in 2000, and 7½ percent below potential in 2001. The deceleration in potential output growth in 1999–2000 implied by trend B seems implausibly large, and the small output gaps inconsistent with the behavior of other macroeconomic data. For instance, consumer prices, purged of the effect of import prices, were increasing through the first half 1998, but began to decline in the fourth quarter of the year and continue to fall through 2001 (see Figure 14, bottom panel).[45] Likewise, unemployment reached its lowest level in the second half of 1998 (only semi-annual data are available) and started increasing thereafter. The evidence thus suggests that, while output was above potential in the first part of 1998, by end-1998 and early 1999, a clear output gap was emerging—consistent with Trend A, but not with Trend B.

According to Trend A, potential growth decreased from 3½ percent per year during 1993–97 to 3 percent by 1998 and 2½ percent thereafter. For the period 1993–2001, potential output growth averaged 3 percent per year—well below the 4½ to 5 percent potential output growth underlying medium-term debt sustainability projections. This may also be compared to Argentina's fitted growth rate implied by the cross-country growth regression reported in Box 8 of the text, which also yields an average growth rate of 3.0 percent per year when the effects of deflation are excluded.[46]

---

[45]The figure shows the residual from an OLS regression of the logarithm of the consumer price index regressed on the logarithm of the import price index.

[46]The model estimated for Box 8 includes a term to capture low or negative inflation, on grounds that deflation may lower aggregate demand. This term is excluded here, since deflation is likely to affect aggregate demand but not potential output.

Appendix II Chronology of Key Developments in 2001–2002

2001

Jan. 12   IMF approves augmentation of Argentina's Stand-By Arrangement to $14 billion and completes second review.

Mar. 2–3   Economy Minister Josehuis Machinea resigns. Ricardo Lopez-Murphy is appointed Minister of Economy.

Mar. 16   Economy Minister Lopez-Murphy announces plan of budget cuts to meet fiscal targets agreed with the IMF.

Mar. 19–20   Economy Minister Lopez-Murphy resigns. Domingo Cavallo is appointed Minister of Economy.

Mar. 26–28   Risk rating agencies lower Argentina's long-term sovereign rating (S&P from BB to B+ and Moody's from B1 to B2).

Mar. 28   Economy Minister Cavallo secures "emergency powers" from Congress. Announces economic program comprising a tax on bank transactions, changes in other taxes and tariffs, and sectoral "competitiveness plans."

April   Central bank reduces liquidity requirements and allows banks to include government securities up to 2 billion pesos among liquidity requirements.

April 16   Minister Cavallo sends to Congress a bill to include the euro in addition to the U.S. dollar in the Convertibility Law.

April 23   Authorities suspend scheduled auction of government bonds.

April 26   Roque Maccarone replaces Pedro Pou as President of the Central Bank.

May 8   Standard & Poor's lowers Argentina's long-term sovereign rating further from B+ to B.

May 21   IMF completes third review of Argentina's Stand-By Arrangement, reprofiling the path for the federal government deficit target during 2001 to accommodate the deviations observed during the first quarter.

June 3   Authorities announce the completion of the "mega-swap." Government bonds with a face value of $29.5 billion are voluntarily exchanged for longer-term instruments.

June 15   Economy Minister Cavallo announces package of tax and trade measures, including a trade compensation mechanism for exporters and importers of non-energy goods.

July 10   Government pays yield of 14.1 percent to place $827 million of 90-day paper.

July 11   Economy Minister Cavallo announces drastic program of fiscal adjustment aimed at eliminating the federal government deficit from August 2001 onwards (the "zero-deficit plan").

July   Risk rating agencies lower Argentina's long-term sovereign rating further (S&P from B to B⁻ and Moody's first from B2 to B3 and then from B3 to Caa1).

July 30   Senate approves the zero-deficit plan (lower house of Congress had approved it on July 20).

Aug. 21   IMF announces likely $8 billion augmentation of Argentina's Stand-By Arrangement credit.

Sept. 7   IMF approves augmentation of stand-by credit to about $21.6 billion and completes Fourth Review.

Sept. 20   The Central Bank activates the contingent repo facility with international banks, boosting gross reserves by about $1.2 billion ($500 million was disbursed in October).

Oct. 9–12   Risk rating agencies lower Argentina's long-term sovereign rating further (S&P from B⁻ to CCC and Moody's from Caa1 to Caa3).

Oct. 14   Ruling coalition obtains less than 25 percent of the votes in mid-term congressional elections.

Oct. 28   Economy Minister Cavallo announces that he will seek a "voluntary" restructuring of all the government debt.

Oct. 30   Standard & Poor's lowers Argentina's long-term sovereign rating from CCC to CC.

Nov. 1	The authorities announce a new fiscal package, including a new batch of competitiveness plans, the rebate of VAT payments on debit card transactions, a temporary reduction in employee social security contributions, a corporate debt restructuring scheme, and a tax amnesty that writes off interest and penalty obligations accrued to end-September 2001.
Nov. 6	Standard & Poor's lowers Argentina's long-term sovereign rating from CC to SD (selective default).
Nov. 23	The central bank introduces an effective cap on bank deposits, by imposing a 100 percent liquidity requirement on deposits paying an interest rate more than 1 percentage point above average of all local banks.
Nov. 26	A Peronist senator, Ramon Puerta, is elected president of the Senate, becoming acting Vice-President of the Republic.
Nov. 30	The authorities announce completion of the local leg of the debt restructuring. Government bonds with a face value of $41 billion at the federal level and $10 billion at the provincial level are "voluntarily" exchanged.
Dec. 1	Facing a substantial run on deposits, the government introduces wide-ranging controls on banking and foreign exchange

transactions, including a weekly 250 pesos cash withdrawal limit on sight accounts.

Dec. 10	The central bank imposes a 98 percent reserve requirement on deposit increases after December 1, 2001, aimed at limiting flight to quality within the system.
Dec. 13	Phase one of the government debt exchange is completed.
Dec. 19	State of emergency is declared to stop protests against Economic Minister Cavallo's economic policies. The lower house of Congress repeals the special legislative powers granted to Cavallo.
Dec. 20	President Fernando de la Rúa and Minister Cavallo resign after days of riots and protests that leave over 20 demonstrators dead. A banking holiday is declared for December 21, extended through December 26. Moody's lowers Argentina ratings to Ca from Caa3.
Dec. 23	Rodríguez Saá is named interim President, announces the default on external debt, and calls presidential elections within 60 days.
Dec. 30	President Rodríguez Saá resigns after his emergency policies are rejected by the Peronist governors.

2002

Jan. 3	Senator Eduardo Duhalde is sworn in as President with a mandate to conclude the remaining period of the de la Rúa presidency; President Duhalde announces the end of convertibility, and the introduction of a dual foreign exchange regime.
Jan. 24	Utility tariffs are frozen indefinitely.
Jan. 30	Emergency law curtailing creditors' rights is approved by Congress (law becomes effective on February 14).
Feb. 4	The government decrees the unification of the exchange rate regime and the asymmetric pesoization of bank balance sheets (assets at 1 peso/U.S.dollar, and liabilities at 1.4 peso per dollar).
Feb. 11	The foreign exchange market opens for the first time under a unified regime; the peso depreciates to 1.8 pesos to the dollar.
Feb. 27	The federal government and the provincial governors reach agreement on a temporary revenue-sharing arrangement that abolishes the minimum floor on transfers to the provinces in exchange for the broadening of the coparticipation base to include the financial transactions tax, and better terms for their debt servicing. The provinces com-

mit to reduce fiscal deficits by 60 percent in 2002 and to achieve balance in 2003.

Mar. 5	Export taxes of 10 percent and 5 percent are imposed on primary products and processed agricultural and industrial products, respectively.
Mar. 8	The pesoization of government debt under Argentine law is decreed.
Mar. 13	A voluntary bond swap (Swap I) is decreed authorizing the exchange of reprogrammed time deposits for government bonds. The decree also authorized issuance of bonds to banks in compensation for the asymmetric pesoization of their balance sheets.
Mar. 25	The peso reaches a peak of 4 pesos per dollar. To contain the depreciation of the currency, the authorities intervene heavily in the foreign exchange market ($800 million in March), tighten the access to central bank liquidity assistance (a matching dollar from the parent being now requested as a condition for assistance to foreign banks), and introduce a variety of exchange regulations affecting banks, foreign exchange bureaus, and exporters. Thirteen new regulations are issued on March 25 alone, bringing the total for the month of March to about 50.

April 9   Export taxes on agricultural primary products are increased to 20 to 23½ percent.

April 19   The central bank suspends for 30 days Scotiabank Quilmes. A bank holiday is declared until Congress approves a solution to the problem of judicial injunctions (*amparos*) releasing bank deposits. The authorities begin working on a plan (the so-called BONEX II plan) to convert reprogrammed time deposits into government bonds.

April 20   Economy Minister Jorge Remes Lenicov presents to congress the BONEX II plan; the draft law is rejected and Minister Remes Lenicov resigns.

April 23   President Duhalde reaches agreement with provincial governors on a 14-point Federal-Provincial Pact.

April 25   Congress approves the Ley Tapón to ease pressure from the amparos. The law modifies court procedures, and states that depositors can only access funds once the judicial process is over; in the meantime funds are deposited in an escrow account.

April 26   Roberto Lavagna, former ambassador to the European Union, is confirmed as the new Minister of Economy.

May 3   The central bank approves the capitalization and liquidity plan for Banco Galicia.

May 6   Exceptions to price indexation for certain types of bank loans and residential leases are decreed. Exempted loans will be adjusted, beginning October 1, 2002, by a wage index (CVS).

May 6   The Federal Congress approves the February Federal-Provincial Pact.

May 15   Congress approves law that reverses the most harmful provisions of the January emergency law and makes limited improvements to the insolvency law.

May 20   The central bank intervenes in Crédit Agricole's Argentine subsidiaries, Banco Bisel, Banco Suquia, and Banco de Entre Ríos. The banks will be administered by Banco de la Nación.

May 30   The Economic Subversion Law is repealed.

May 31   In order to tighten the control over the sale of export receipts, the central bank announces that dollar export revenues in excess of $1 million will have to be sold directly to the central bank.

May 31   Province of Buenos Aires and federal government sign full-fledged text of Bilateral Agreement. Agreement on the Annexes (quarterly fiscal targets and calendar for disbursement) is reached in June.

June 1   President Duhalde signs the Options Plan on reprogrammed deposits, a revised version of former Minister Remes' BONEX II Plan, giving depositors the option to exchange deposits into bonds.

June 12   Senate approves draft law limiting foreign ownership in the media to 30 percent of capital.

June 18   The minimum level of export proceeds that should be surrendered to the central bank lowered from $1 million to $500,000.

June 21   Central bank President Mario Blejer resigns.

June 25   Central bank Vice-President Aldo Pignanelli appointed central bank president.

June 26   A second level court rules the Ley Tapón unconstitutional.

June 26   Two demonstrators shot dead by the police; worst riots since December 2001.

July 2   Representatives of trade unions and businesses agree to raise private sector wages by 100 pesos a month effective July 1, and the monthly minimum wage is raised from 250 pesos to 350 pesos.

July 2   President Duhalde moves the presidential election forward to March 2003, from September 2003.

July 9   In response to a class action suit lodged by the country's ombudsman on behalf of all depositors, a federal court declares the deposit freeze and pesoization unconstitutional.

July 19   Banca Nazionale del Lavoro (BNL) announces that it will gradually withdraw from Argentina.

July 24   The government issues a decree suspending court-ordered withdrawals of frozen bank deposits for 120 business days.

July 25   The decree suspending deposit withdrawals obtained through court orders is declared partially unconstitutional by a federal judge.

July 26   Following a demand by the national ombudsman a judge rules unconstitutional the government decree suspending lawsuits on December's bank curbs for 120 business days.

July 29   A panel of monetary policy experts makes public several proposals to resolve the country's financial crisis, including a monetary policy anchor, an independent central bank, the ending of peso printing deficit-financing, and an end to the use of quasi-currencies by the provinces. The report calls for a floating exchange rate and urges Argentina to stop using international reserves to support the peso.

Aug. 9	Central bank director and superintendent of banks Felipe Murolo resigns.
Aug. 15	Congress approves a bill extending for 90 days (through mid-November 2002) the provision that suspends certain kinds of creditor-initiated nonbankruptcy law enforcement actions. Congress also approves a bill extending for 60 days (through end-September 2002) the application of price indexation to loans.
Aug. 22	The Supreme Court declares unconstitutional the 13 percent salary cut for federal government workers and pensioners, implemented from July 2001.
Aug. 23	A federal court declares the open primary elections (where all registered voters can participate) planned for November unconstitutional.
Aug. 26	The government postpones to December 15 (from end-November) the date set for the primaries for presidential elections in order to allow more time to rewrite voting rules.
Aug. 26	The government issues a resolution to allow the issuance of bank-compensation bonds for the asymmetric pesoization.
Aug. 28	A federal court establishes that parent banks should be fully responsible for the liabilities of subsidiaries in Argentina.
Sept. 3	The government introduces new exchange controls in an attempt to boost international reserves and defend the peso: (1) the limit for exporters' foreign exchange surrender to the central bank is reduced from $500,000 to $200,000; (2) the minimum maturity of external debt contracted by private nonfinancial entities is set to 90 days; (3) exchange bureaus are required to deposit with the central bank foreign exchange holdings exceeding $1.5 million on a daily basis; and (4) the net dollar positions held by exchange dealers operating on behalf of the central bank are reduced by an average 40 percent.
Sept. 5	The federal administrative dispute chamber, an appellate court, rules that the decrees establishing the *corralito* and pesoization, were unconstitutional. The ruling applies to only one case but opens the door for further similar rulings.
Sept. 9	Further tightening of foreign exchange controls: prior authorization from the central bank for dollar purchases exceeding $100,000 for portfolio and other financial investments abroad, as well as for the purchase of foreign banknotes.
Sept. 13	The Federal Court of Appeals declares the *corralito*, pesoization, and the 120 days suspension of executions against the *corralito*, unconstitutional; the decision allows depositors to claim their deposits in court

	immediately. The 2003 budget is submitted to Congress.
Sept. 17	The government issues a decree that extends the negotiation period for utility tariffs for another 120 days with the possibility of a further 60 days extension.
Sept. 20	The government launches a second swap of bonds for frozen deposits and announces the easing of restrictions on frozen time-deposits of up to 7,000 pesos.
Oct. 31	The monthly cash withdrawal limit on the *corralito* is raised to 2,000 pesos from 1,200 pesos.
Nov. 11	After discussions with the government, the banks announce a voluntary 75-day stay on foreclosures.
Nov. 14	The government falls short of meeting an $809 million World Bank debt payment; only $79.2 million in interest is paid.
Nov. 14	President Duhalde signs a decree lowering the VAT rate by 2 percentage points to 19 percent for two months.
Nov. 15	A lower court suspends the public hearings designed to grant a tariff increase to the privatized utility companies.
Nov. 18	President Duhalde signs a 12-point agreement with provincial governors and some key legislators over the new election timetable and the government's economic policies.
Nov. 21	The Senate approves President Duhalde's plans for delaying the presidential election by a month to April. The first round of presidential elections is scheduled to be held on April 27, 2003, and will be followed by a second round on May 10, if necessary.
Nov. 22	The government announces that it will lift the remaining *corralito* restrictions on sight accounts effective December 2. Term deposits (the *corralón*) remain frozen.
Nov. 22	Minister Lavagna submits a draft decree to President Duhalde lifting the tariff rates on electricity and natural gas. On average, electricity rates will rise 9.0 percent and natural gas 7.2 percent.
Nov. 27	Executive decree issued, authorizing court-imposed stay on foreclosures for 30 business days, during which time mediation is required.
Dec. 9	The resignation of central bank President Pignanelli is accepted by President Duhalde.
Dec. 10	President Duhalde appoints Alfonso Prat Gay to be central bank president. Legislation eliminating the ability of the executive to grant tax amnesties becomes effective.
Dec. 11	A court order reverses the decreed increases in electricity and gas tariffs.

References

Alesina, Alberto, and Roberto Perotti, 1995, "Taxation and Redistribution in an Open Economy," *European Economic Review,* Vol. 39 (May), pp. 961–79.

Alesina, Alberto, Ricardo Hausmann, Rudolf Hommes, and Ernesto Stein, 1996, "Budget Institutions and Fiscal Performance in Latin America," NBER Working Paper No. 5586 (Cambridge, MA: National Bureau of Economic Research).

Blanchard, Olivier, and Augustin Landier, 2001, "The Perverse Effects of Partial Labor Market Reform: Fixed Duration Contracts in France," NBER Working Paper No. 8219 (Cambridge, MA: National Bureau of Economic Research).

Caballero, Ricardo, and Arvind Krishnamurthy, 2002, "A Dual Liquidity Model for Emerging Markets," *American Economic Review: Papers and Proceedings,* Vol. 92, No. 2 (May), pp. 33–37.

Calmfors, Lars, and John Drifill, 1988, "Bargaining Structure, Corporatism, and Macroeconomic Performance," *Economic Policy,* Vol. 3, No. 1.

Calvo, Guillermo, 2002, "Sudden Stops, the Real Exchange Rate and Fiscal Sustainability" (unpublished; Washington: Inter-American Development Bank).

Canzoneri, Matthew, Robert Cumby, and Behzad Diba, 1998, "Fiscal Discipline and Exchange Rate Regimes," CEPR Discussion Paper No. 1899 (London: Centre for Economic Policy Research).

Card, David, and Richard Freeman, 2002, "What Have Two Decades of British Economic Reform Delivered?" NBER Working Paper No. 8801 (Cambridge, MA: National Bureau of Economic Research).

Chudnovsky, Daniel, Andres Lopez, and Fernando Porta, 1996, "Intra-Industry Trade and Regional Integration: The Case of the Auto Industry in Argentina," in *Latin American Trade in Manufactures: A Handbook of Regional and Country Cases,* ed. by M. Lord (Ann Arbor: University of Michigan Press).

Collyns, Charles, and Russell Kincaid, eds., 2003, *Managing Financial Crises: Recent Experience and Lessons for Latin America,* IMF Occasional Paper No. 217 (Washington: International Monetary Fund).

Cuevas, Alfredo, 2003, "Reforming Intergovernmental Fiscal Relations in Argentina," IMF Working Paper No. 03/90 (Washington: International Monetary Fund).

De la Torre, Augusto, Eduardo Yeyati, and Sergio Schmukler, 2002, "Argentina's Financial Crisis: Floating Money, Sinking Banking" (unpublished; Washington: World Bank).

Di Tella, Rafael, and Robert MacCulloch, 1998, "The Consequences of Labor Market Flexibility: Panel Evidence Based on Survey Data," ZEI Working Paper.

Duguay, Pierre, 1994, "Empirical Evidence on the Strength of the Monetary Transmission Mechanism in Canada: An Aggregate Approach," *Journal of Monetary Economics,* Vol. 33 (February), pp. 39–61.

Edwards, Sebastian, and Alejandra Cox Edwards, 2000, "Economic Reforms and Labor Markets: Policy Issues and Lessons from Chile," NBER Working Paper No. 7646 (Cambridge, MA: National Bureau of Economic Research).

Feldstein, Martin, 2002, "Lessons from Argentina" (unpublished; Cambridge, MA: Harvard University).

Galiani, Sebastian, 2001, "Labor Market Reform in Argentina: Where Do We Stand?" (unpublished; Buenos Aires, Universidad de San Andres, November).

———, and Hugo Hopenhayn, 2003, "Duration and Risk of Unemployment in Argentina," *Journal of Development Economics,* Vol. 71, pp. 199–212.

Ghosh, Atish, Anne Marie Gulde, and Holger Wolf, 2002, *Exchange Rate Regimes: Choices and Consequences* (Cambridge, MA: MIT Press).

Ghosh, Atish, Timothy Lane, Marianne Schulze-Ghattas, Aleš Bulíř, Javier Hamann, and Alex Mourmouras, 2002, *IMF-Supported Programs in Capital Account Crises,* IMF Occasional Paper No. 210 (Washington: International Monetary Fund).

Ghosh, Atish, and Steven Phillips, 1998, "Warning: Inflation May Be Harmful to Your Growth," *IMF Staff Papers,* International Monetary Fund, Vol. 45 (December), pp. 672-710.

Gruber, Jonathan, 1995, "The Incidence of Payroll Taxation: Evidence from Chile," *Journal of Labor Economics,* Vol. 15 (July), pp. 72–101.

Hausmann, Ricardo, and Andrés Velasco, 2002, "The Argentine Collapse: Hard Money's Soft Underbelly" (unpublished; Cambridge, MA: Harvard University).

Heckman, James, and Carmen Pagés, 2000, "The Cost of Job Security Regulation: Evidence from Latin American Labor Markets," NBER Working Paper No. 7773 (Cambridge, MA: National Bureau of Economic Research).

Hirschman, Albert O., 1985, "Reflections on the Latin American Experience," in *The Politics of Inflation and Economic Stagnation,* ed. by Leon Lindberg and Charles Maier (Washington: Brookings Institution).

Hopenhayn, Hugo, 2001, "Labor Market Policies and Employment Duration: the Effects of Labor Market Reform in Argentina" (unpublished; Washington: Inter-American Development Bank, February).

IMF, 2002a, "Assessing Sustainability," available via the Internet at *www.imf.org/external/np/pdr/sus/2002/eng/052802.htm.*

———, 2002b, "IMF Executive Board Reviews the Fund's Surveillance," Public Information Notice No. 02/44. Available via the Internet at *www.imf.org/external/np/sec/pn/2002/pn0244.htm.*

Lane, Timothy, Atish Ghosh, Javier Hamann, Steven Phillips, Marianne Schulze-Ghattas, and Tsidi Tsikata, 1999, *IMF-Supported Programs in Indonesia, Korea, and Thailand: A Preliminary Assessment,* IMF Occasional Paper No. 178 (Washington: International Monetary Fund).

Levine, David, and Laura D'Andrea Tyson, 1990, "Participation, Productivity and the Firm's Environment," in *Paying for Productivity: A Look at the Evidence,* ed. by Alan S. Blinder (Washington: Brookings Institution).

Mussa, Michael, 2002, *Argentina and the Fund: from Triumph to Tragedy,* Policy Analysis in International Economics 67 (Washington: Institute for International Economics).

Nickel, Stephen, and Kevin Denny, 1990, "Unions and Investment in British Industry," University of Oxford Discussion Paper (Oxford, U.K.).

Perry, Guillermo, and Luis Serven, 2002, "The Anatomy and Physiology of a Multiple Crisis: Why Was Argentina Special and What Can We Learn from It?" (unpublished; Washington: World Bank).

Roubini, Nouriel, 2001, "Should Argentina Dollarize or Float? The Pros and Cons of Alternative Exchange Rate Regimes and Their Implications for Domestic and Foreign Debt Restructuring/Reduction," Stern School of Business draft Working Paper (New York: New York University).

Stiglitz, Joseph, 2002, "Argentina, Shortchanged," *The Washington Post,* May 12.

Thomas, Alun, 2002, "The Costs and Benefits of Various Wage Bargaining Structures: An Empirical Exploration," IMF Working Paper No. 02/71 (Washington: International Monetary Fund).

Yeats, Alexander, 1998, "Does Mercosur's Trade Performance Raise Concerns About the Effects of Regional Trade Arrangements?" *The World Bank Economic Review,* Vol. 12, No. 1.

Woodford, Michael, 1994, "Monetary Policy and Price Level Determinacy in a Cash-in-Advance Economy," *Economic Theory,* Vol. 4, No. 3, pp. 345–80.

———, 1995, "Price Level Determinacy Without Control of a Monetary Aggregate," *Carnegie-Rochester Conference Series on Public Policy,* Vol. 43, pp. 1–53.

Recent Occasional Papers of the International Monetary Fund

236. Lessons from the Crisis in Argentina, by Christina Daseking, Atish R. Ghosh, Alun Thomas, and Timothy Lane. 2004.

235. A New Look at Exchange Rate Volatility and Trade Flows, by Peter B. Clark, Natalia Tamirisa, and Shang-Jin Wei, with Azim Sadikov and Li Zeng. 2004.

234. Adopting the Euro in Central Europe: Challenges of the Next Step in European Integration, by Susan Schadler, Paulo Drummond, Louis Kuijs, Zuzana Murgasova, and Rachel van Elkan. 2004.

233. Germany's Three-Pillar Banking System: Cross-Country Perspectives in Europe, by Allan Brunner, Jörg Decressin, Daniel Hardy, and Beata Kudela. 2004.

232. China's Growth and Integration into the World Economy: Prospects and Challenges, edited by Eswar Prasad. 2004.

231. Chile: Policies and Institutions Underpinning Stability and Growth, by Eliot Kalter, Steven Phillips, Marco A. Espinosa-Vega, Rodolfo Luzio, Mauricio Villafuerte, and Manmohan Singh. 2004.

230. Financial Stability in Dollarized Countries, by Anne-Marie Gulde, David Hoelscher, Alain Ize, David Marston, and Gianni De Nicoló. 2004.

229. Evolution and Performance of Exchange Rate Regimes, by Kenneth S. Rogoff, Aasim M. Husain, Ashoka Mody, Robin Brooks, and Nienke Oomes. 2004.

228. Capital Markets and Financial Intermediation in The Baltics, by Alfred Schipke, Christian Beddies, Susan M. George, and Niamh Sheridan. 2004.

227. U.S. Fiscal Policies and Priorities for Long-Run Sustainability, edited by Martin Mühleisen and Christopher Towe. 2004.

226. Hong Kong SAR: Meeting the Challenges of Integration with the Mainland, edited by Eswar Prasad, with contributions from Jorge Chan-Lau, Dora Iakova, William Lee, Hong Liang, Ida Liu, Papa N'Diaye, and Tao Wang. 2004.

225. Rules-Based Fiscal Policy in France, Germany, Italy, and Spain, by Teresa Dában, Enrica Detragiache, Gabriel di Bella, Gian Maria Milesi-Ferretti, and Steven Symansky. 2003.

224. Managing Systemic Banking Crises, by a staff team led by David S. Hoelscher and Marc Quintyn. 2003.

223. Monetary Union Among Member Countries of the Gulf Cooperation Council, by a staff team led by Ugo Fasano. 2003.

222. Informal Funds Transfer Systems: An Analysis of the Informal Hawala System, by Mohammed El Qorchi, Samuel Munzele Maimbo, and John F. Wilson. 2003.

221. Deflation: Determinants, Risks, and Policy Options, by Manmohan S. Kumar. 2003.

220. Effects of Financial Globalization on Developing Countries: Some Empirical Evidence, by Eswar S. Prasad, Kenneth Rogoff, Shang-Jin Wei, and Ayhan Kose. 2003.

219. Economic Policy in a Highly Dollarized Economy: The Case of Cambodia, by Mario de Zamaroczy and Sopanha Sa. 2003.

218. Fiscal Vulnerability and Financial Crises in Emerging Market Economies, by Richard Hemming, Michael Kell, and Axel Schimmelpfennig. 2003.

217. Managing Financial Crises: Recent Experience and Lessons for Latin America, edited by Charles Collyns and G. Russell Kincaid. 2003.

216. Is the PRGF Living Up to Expectations?—An Assessment of Program Design, by Sanjeev Gupta, Mark Plant, Benedict Clements, Thomas Dorsey, Emanuele Baldacci, Gabriela Inchauste, Shamsuddin Tareq, and Nita Thacker. 2002.

215. Improving Large Taxpayers' Compliance: A Review of Country Experience, by Katherine Baer. 2002.

214. Advanced Country Experiences with Capital Account Liberalization, by Age Bakker and Bryan Chapple. 2002.

213. The Baltic Countries: Medium-Term Fiscal Issues Related to EU and NATO Accession, by Johannes Mueller, Christian Beddies, Robert Burgess, Vitali Kramarenko, and Joannes Mongardini. 2002.

212. Financial Soundness Indicators: Analytical Aspects and Country Practices, by V. Sundararajan, Charles Enoch, Armida San José, Paul Hilbers, Russell Krueger, Marina Moretti, and Graham Slack. 2002.

211. Capital Account Liberalization and Financial Sector Stability, by a staff team led by Shogo Ishii and Karl Habermeier. 2002.

210. IMF-Supported Programs in Capital Account Crises, by Atish Ghosh, Timothy Lane, Marianne Schulze-Ghattas, Aleš Bulíř, Javier Hamann, and Alex Mourmouras. 2002.

209. Methodology for Current Account and Exchange Rate Assessments, by Peter Isard, Hamid Faruqee, G. Russell Kincaid, and Martin Fetherston. 2001.

208. Yemen in the 1990s: From Unification to Economic Reform, by Klaus Enders, Sherwyn Williams, Nada Choueiri, Yuri Sobolev, and Jan Walliser. 2001.

207. Malaysia: From Crisis to Recovery, by Kanitta Meesook, Il Houng Lee, Olin Liu, Yougesh Khatri, Natalia Tamirisa, Michael Moore, and Mark H. Krysl. 2001.

206. The Dominican Republic: Stabilization, Structural Reform, and Economic Growth, by a staff team led by Philip Young comprising Alessandro Giustiniani, Werner C. Keller, and Randa E. Sab and others. 2001.

205. Stabilization and Savings Funds for Nonrenewable Resources, by Jeffrey Davis, Rolando Ossowski, James Daniel, and Steven Barnett. 2001.

204. Monetary Union in West Africa (ECOWAS): Is It Desirable and How Could It Be Achieved? by Paul Masson and Catherine Pattillo. 2001.

203. Modern Banking and OTC Derivatives Markets: The Transformation of Global Finance and Its Implications for Systemic Risk, by Garry J. Schinasi, R. Sean Craig, Burkhard Drees, and Charles Kramer. 2000.

202. Adopting Inflation Targeting: Practical Issues for Emerging Market Countries, by Andrea Schaechter, Mark R. Stone, and Mark Zelmer. 2000.

201. Developments and Challenges in the Caribbean Region, by Samuel Itam, Simon Cueva, Erik Lundback, Janet Stotsky, and Stephen Tokarick. 2000.

200. Pension Reform in the Baltics: Issues and Prospects, by Jerald Schiff, Niko Hobdari, Axel Schimmelpfennig, and Roman Zytek. 2000.

199. Ghana: Economic Development in a Democratic Environment, by Sérgio Pereira Leite, Anthony Pellechio, Luisa Zanforlin, Girma Begashaw, Stefania Fabrizio, and Joachim Harnack. 2000.

198. Setting Up Treasuries in the Baltics, Russia, and Other Countries of the Former Soviet Union: An Assessment of IMF Technical Assistance, by Barry H. Potter and Jack Diamond. 2000.

197. Deposit Insurance: Actual and Good Practices, by Gillian G.H. Garcia. 2000.

196. Trade and Trade Policies in Eastern and Southern Africa, by a staff team led by Arvind Subramanian, with Enrique Gelbard, Richard Harmsen, Katrin Elborgh-Woytek, and Piroska Nagy. 2000.

195. The Eastern Caribbean Currency Union—Institutions, Performance, and Policy Issues, by Frits van Beek, José Roberto Rosales, Mayra Zermeño, Ruby Randall, and Jorge Shepherd. 2000.

194. Fiscal and Macroeconomic Impact of Privatization, by Jeffrey Davis, Rolando Ossowski, Thomas Richardson, and Steven Barnett. 2000.

193. Exchange Rate Regimes in an Increasingly Integrated World Economy, by Michael Mussa, Paul Masson, Alexander Swoboda, Esteban Jadresic, Paolo Mauro, and Andy Berg. 2000. 192. Macroprudential Indicators of Financial System Soundness, by a staff team led by Owen Evans, Alfredo M. Leone, Mahinder Gill, and Paul Hilbers. 2000.

191. Social Issues in IMF-Supported Programs, by Sanjeev Gupta, Louis Dicks-Mireaux, Ritha Khemani, Calvin McDonald, and Marijn Verhoeven. 2000.

Note: For information on the titles and availability of Occasional Papers not listed, please consult the IMF's *Publications Catalog* or contact IMF Publication Services.